Fantastic Wood Toys You Can Make

•••••

Joe B. Hicks

 Sterling Publishing Co., Inc.   New York

DEDICATION

This book is dedicated to those people in my life who have been most instrumental in the development of the toys found herein, my family. To my children Mike, David, Matt and Jodi, who are a constant source of ideas and energy, and to my wonderful wife, Mary, who supports, encourages and works with me day after day.

Edited by Carol Palmer

Library of Congress Cataloging-in-Publication Data

Hicks, Joe B.
    Fantastic wood toys you can make.

    Includes index.
    1. Wooden toy making.   I. Title.
TT174.5.W6H53   1988   688.7′2   88-2145
ISBN 0-8069-6674-2 (pbk.)

1   3   5   7   9   10   8   6   4   2

Copyright © 1988 by Joe B. Hicks
Published by Sterling Publishing Co., Inc.
Two Park Avenue, New York, N.Y. 10016
Distributed in Canada by Oak Tree Press Ltd.
% Canadian Manda Group, P.O. Box 920, Station U
Toronto, Ontario, Canada M8Z 5P9
Distributed in the United Kingdom by Blandford Press
Link House, West Street, Poole, Dorset BH15 1LL, England
Distributed in Australia by Capricorn Ltd.
P.O. Box 665, Lane Cove, NSW 2066
Manufactured in the United States of America
All rights reserved

Contents

Color Section Follows Page 64

Introduction

Remember when you were a child, how you could remove yourself from the world of reality and put yourself into worlds of your own making—into worlds of fantasy? You could create imaginary ships to sail imaginary seas. You could cause yourself to fly high above the earth on wings made only of thought. You could build fortresses, caves, mountains and rivers, and even create friends and foes. Remember how these things became so real to you? You could see them and touch them. You could talk with them and even love them. All of the wonderful things that you did in your mind were done through the power of imagination.

Imagination is a wonderful gift. It can be used to bring children hours of pleasure and excitement. It can seed the thoughts that actually put men into outer space. It is the reason why today we drive automobiles for transportation rather than walking or riding horses. Imagination is the key to creativity.

Unfortunately, we usually associate the imaginative process with children. This is probably because that is where we find it most active. Children aren't burdened by heavy thoughts, plans and worries, so imagination for them is spontaneous. However, our busy world of today leaves us little time to escape the things of reality, such as busy work schedules and social activities. These are of utmost importance to our families' financial well-being and to our careers; however, somewhere hidden away deep in the dusty, unused corners of our minds there lies a spark of life—a spark that waits patiently to be fanned into the flame of creativity.

For some of us, when that spark ignites, it brings us into the fantasy world of wooden toys. Out of that world flows toy trucks and airplanes, ships and doll houses, rocking horses and tractors, and countless other items that once were only small, unkindled sparks within our minds. These toys bring pleasure and joy not only to the children of our world, but the builders as well. There are few things more special than to see the bright smile and feel the warm joy of a child with a new toy. It is especially good when you know that you created that toy with your own hands. But the feelings cannot be described when you see that child keep and protect that toy for years to come because you made it for him.

This book has been designed and written for those who express their imagination and creative talents in this way.

The imaginative toy builder is not required to have reached a particular level of expertise or skill, or to have learned to produce a predetermined quantity of items from his shop in a short time. He is simply one who has learned to fan the spark of imagination into the flame of creativity and make someone happy in the process. The toy builder is limited only by his imagination, for if he can imagine a thing, he can find a way to build it.

The following pages will share some toys designed and built by the author. These particular designs have been chosen for this book because they cover various degrees of difficulty from very basic to moderately challenging. They also cover a wide range of interest, from rocking horses to space ships and from play kitchens to planes.

Each of the projects have been carefully drawn to show exact dimensions. Many of the toy layouts are too large to reproduce in this book full size. They have been reduced and printed on top of grids. To enlarge these drawings back to their original size, use 1″ (25.4 mm) grid paper. Draw a portion of the original pattern one square at a time: make the line running through the 1″ (25.4 mm) grid correspond directly to the line running through the book's smaller square. The instructions are meant to be as easily understood as possible. The step-by-step photos should be helpful in your understanding of the construction process.

The tools most commonly found in home workshops will be all you'll need to build any of the projects included here. The only major bench tools needed are a table saw and/or a radial arm saw, and a bandsaw or jigsaw. A drill press will be helpful at times, but not essential. A hand-held router, finish sander and drill motor will also be helpful. Then, of course, you'll need the basic hand tools such as a hammer, screwdriver and an adjustable wrench.

The instructions for each toy will include a list of the materials and supplies needed to build that toy. However, you should start out with a good supply of carpenter's glue and an assortment of finishing nails.

As you begin to get involved in these projects, you will see that some of the basic design concepts are repeated from one project to another. With this understanding, it is entirely possible that you could employ some of the design concepts and create your own designs and custom-built items.

You will also soon see that wooden toys can vary in design from a very basic profile toy, with only a few pieces cut into simple shapes, to actual scale models. The projects here have not gone to the latter extreme, but if you find that thought challenging, pursue it.

METRIC SYSTEM

Chapter 1
The Little House

Illus. 1.1

Any young child would be delighted to receive this gift and would be thrilled to set it up as a dollhouse or use it as "army headquarters" or a farmhouse.

The project should take you a couple of days to build. Painting and decorating may increase that time frame somewhat. If the young recipient is allowed to participate in the construction and decorating of this house you'll probably throw out any time schedule anyway, but the two of you will have a lot of fun together. He or she is sure to cherish this gift and remember those hours spent together with you for many years to come.

Remember safety. Turn off tools and unplug them with children around the shop. Never leave the child unattended in the shop, and explain the hazards to them in a way that they can understand.

Materials List

¼" (6.35 mm) veneer plywood, ½ sheet
½" (12.7 mm) veneer plywood, ⅛ sheet
¾" (19 mm) solid stock, 1" ×
   4" (2.54 × 10.16 cm) .... 2½ linear ft.
                 (7.6 meters)
⅛" (3.18 mm) hardwood
   dowel .... 36" (91 cm)
1/16" (1.6 mm) balsa wood
   sheeting .... 1 sheet 4" ×
                 36" (10 cm ×
                 91 cm)
¾" (19 mm) wire brads ..... small box
Carpenter's glue .... small bottle
Nontoxic paint: your choice of colors in small containers

Cutting List

Part 1 ... First Floor .... Make 1
Part 2 ... Second Floor .... Make 1
Part 3 ... Front Wall .... Make 1
Part 4 ... End Wall .... Make 2
Part 5 ... Lower Interior Wall .... Make 1
Part 6 ... Upper Interior Wall .... Make 1
Part 7 ... Front Roof Section ..... Make 1
Part 8 ... Rear Roof Section ..... Make 1
Part 9 ... Porch Roof Section ..... Make 2
Part 10 .. Stairs .... Make 1
Part 11 .. Porch Gable .... Make 2

Note: The upper edges of all four roof sections are cut at a 30° bevel to allow the roof to fit together properly.

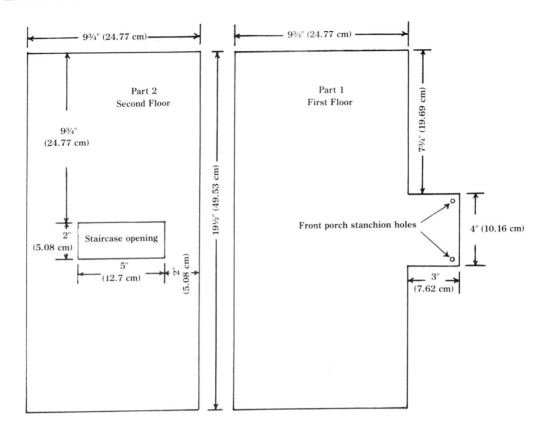

Illus. 1.2 Floor sections.

Illus. 1.3 Roof sections.

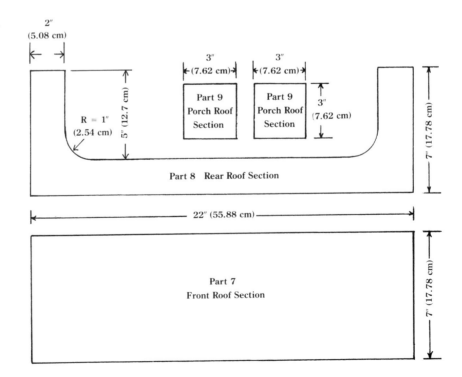

Instructions

LAYOUT

1. Lay out and cut the two floor pieces (Parts 1 and 2) from ½″ (12.7 mm) veneer plywood (Illus. 1.2).

2. Locate and cut the stairwell opening in the second floor (Part 2).

3. On the first floor (Part 1) locate the two front porch stanchion holes at ⅜″ (9.5 mm) from each side and ⅜″ (9.5 mm) from the front of the porch, and drill using a ¼″ (6.35 mm) drill. Drill them about halfway through the floor piece.

4. Sand these parts well and set them aside.

5. Using ¼″ (6.35 mm) plywood, lay out and cut all of the wall and roof parts (Illus. 1.3, 1.5, and 1.6).

6. To cut out the window openings in the wall sections, first drill a small hole, then use a scroll saw or coping saw to cut to shape.

7. Sand all of these parts well and set them aside.

STAIR ASSEMBLY

8. Refer to Illus. 1.4 showing the stairs (Part 10). The stairs are made from a solid block of wood 2″ (5.08 cm) thick and approximately 4″ × 10″ (10.16 cm × 25.4 cm). This block can be obtained by laminating three pieces of ¾″ (19 mm) stock together

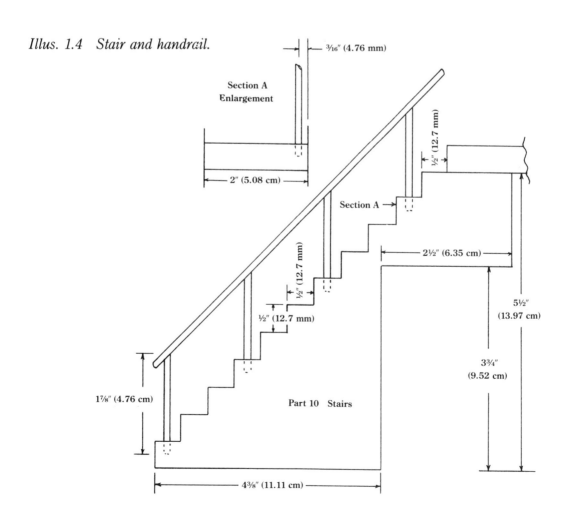

Illus. 1.4   Stair and handrail.

Section A
Enlargement

³⁄₁₆″ (4.76 mm)

2″ (5.08 cm)

½″ (12.7 mm)

Section A

½″ (12.7 mm)

½″ (12.7 mm)

½″ (12.7 mm)

2½″ (6.35 cm)

5½″ (13.97 cm)

3¾″ (9.52 cm)

1⅞″ (4.76 cm)

Part 10   Stairs

4⅜″ (11.11 cm)

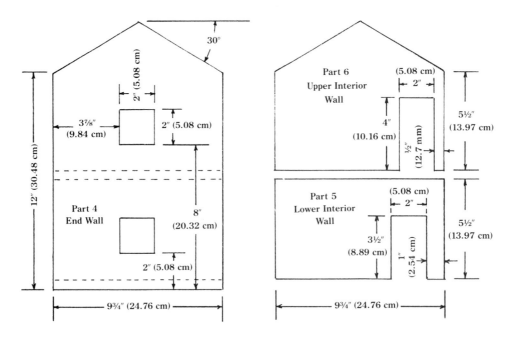

Illus. 1.5   Wall sections.

Illus. 1.6   Front wall, Part 3.

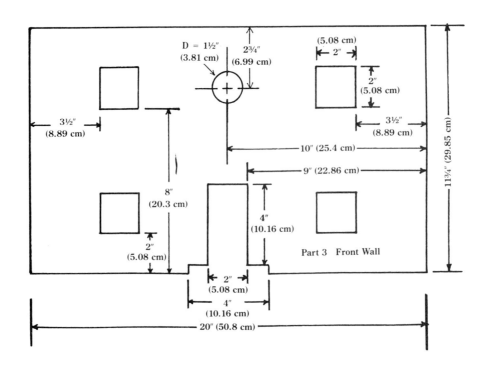

and then ripping to exactly 2″ (5.08 cm) in thickness.

9. Now, lay out the stairs on this block and cut to shape with a bandsaw.

10. Sand the stair part and set it aside.

PORCH

11. Referring to Illus. 1.7, lay out and cut two of the porch gables, Part 11, from ¾″ (19 mm) stock.

12. Drill the two stanchion holes into the bottom of one of the gable parts. Drill to a depth of ⅛″ (3.2 mm).

13. Assembly can now begin by attaching the front wall (Part 3) and the two end walls (Part 4) to the first floor (Part 1).

14. Secure these walls to the first floor with carpenter's glue and ¾″ (19 mm) wire brads (Illus. 1.8).

15. Secure the corners where the walls intersect in the same manner.

16. Using carpenter's glue, secure the porch gable without the stanchion holes to the front wall (Part 1). Center it directly above the front door and locate it 4½″ (11.43 cm)

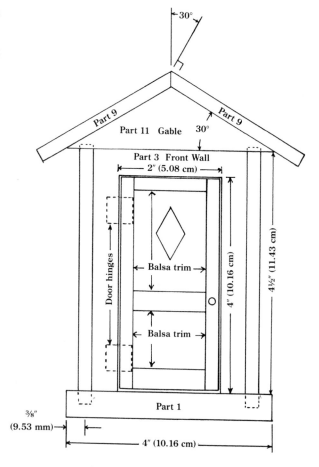

Illus. 1.7   Door and porch.

Illus. 1.8   Secure the walls to the first floor. Install the front porch gable.

Illus. 1.9   Install the front roof section and front porch roof.

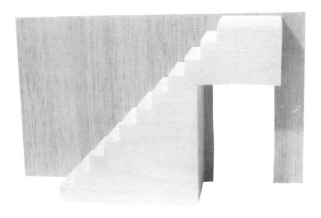

Illus. 1.10   Secure the stairs to the lower interior wall.

Illus. 1.11   Build the staircase handrail using ⅛″ (3.2 mm) doweling.

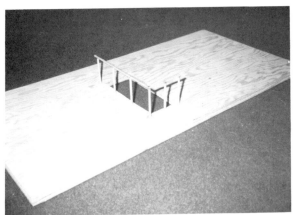

Illus. 1.12   Build the second floor handrail using ⅛″ (3.2 mm) doweling.

Illus. 1.13   Install the upper interior wall section flush with the left side of the stairwell opening as viewed from the rear of the dollhouse.

Illus. 1.14   Install the rear roof section.

Illus. 1.15   Round window.

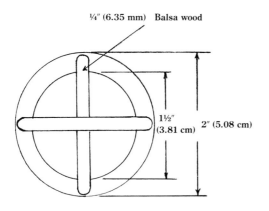

¼" (6.35 mm) Balsa wood

1½"
(3.81 cm)   2" (5.08 cm)

Illus. 1.16   Window details.

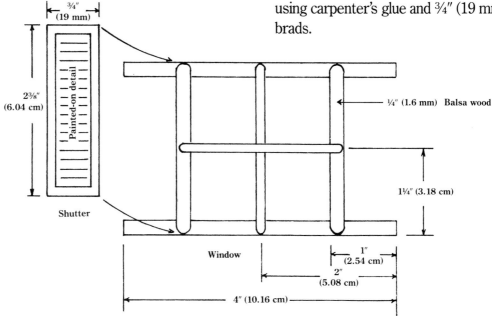

¾"
(19 mm)

2⅜"
(6.04 cm)

Painted-on detail

¼" (1.6 mm) Balsa wood

1¼" (3.18 cm)

Shutter

Window

1"
(2.54 cm)

2"
(5.08 cm)

4" (10.16 cm)

from the porch floor. Be sure the bottom side of the gable is level (Illus. 1.9).

17. Cut two ¼" (6.35 mm) dowels to a length of 4⅞" (12.38 cm).

18. Using the two dowels and carpenter's glue, erect the other porch gable (Part 11) and align it with the first one.

19. Glue on the porch roof sections (Part 9) with the beveled sides intersecting at the top as indicated in Illus. 1.7 and Illus. 1.9.

ASSEMBLY

20. Install the front roof section (Part 7) using carpenter's glue and ¾" (19 mm) wire brads.

21. Locate and secure the stairs (Part 10) to the lower interior wall (Part 5) with carpenter's glue (Illus. 1.10).

22. Build the staircase handrail as shown in Illus. 1.6 using ⅛" (3.2 mm) dowel and carpenter's glue (Illus. 1.11).

23. Build the handrail around the two exposed sides of the stairwell opening on the second floor (Part 2) in the same way (Illus. 1.12).

24. Install the lower interior wall assembly using carpenter's glue and ¾" (19 mm) wire brads.

Illus. 1.17   Windows and shutters are made from ⅟₁₆″ (1.6 mm) balsa-wood material.

NOTE: Viewing the house from the rear, the right side of this wall should be located exactly 7½″ (19.05 cm) from the inside of the right end wall.

25. Mark the end walls and the front wall on the inside at several locations exactly 6″ (15.24 cm) from the top surface of the first floor. These will be location and leveling marks for the second floor.

26. Now, using these marks as guides, secure the second floor in place with carpenter's glue and ¾″ (19 mm) wire brads.
    NOTE: Be sure the floor section is turned so that the stairwell opening is directly above the staircase.

27. Now, install the upper interior wall section (Part 6) flush with the left side of the stairwell opening (Illus. 1.13), using glue and ¾″ (19 mm) wire brads.

28. Install the rear roof section (Part 8) with glue and ¾″ (19 mm) brads (Illus. 1.14).

29. This is a good time to paint the completed assembly. Use nontoxic paint of your color choice.

FRONT DOOR

30. To make the front door, simply cut a piece of ¼″ (6.35 mm) plywood to a 2″ × 4″ (5.08 cm × 10.16 cm) size and decorate it as shown in Illus. 1.7 with strips of ⅟₁₆″ (1.6 mm) balsa wood.

31. The door hinges are two small pieces of fairly heavy cloth glued in place under the balsa wood. The door should swing to the outside.

32. Paint the door to coordinate with the house colors.

33. The doorknob can be a plastic pin head.

WINDOWS

34. The windows and shutters are also made with ⅟₁₆″ (1.6 mm) balsa wood glued together as shown in Illus. 1.15, 1.16 and 1.17.

35. Paint the windows and shutters to coordinate with the house colors before installing them.

36. Install the window and shutters with carpenter's glue.

This completes the construction of your new house. I'm sure its new owner will find hours of pleasure in furnishing and decorating it.

Chapter 2
The Rocking Horse

Scale 1″ (2.54 cm) per square

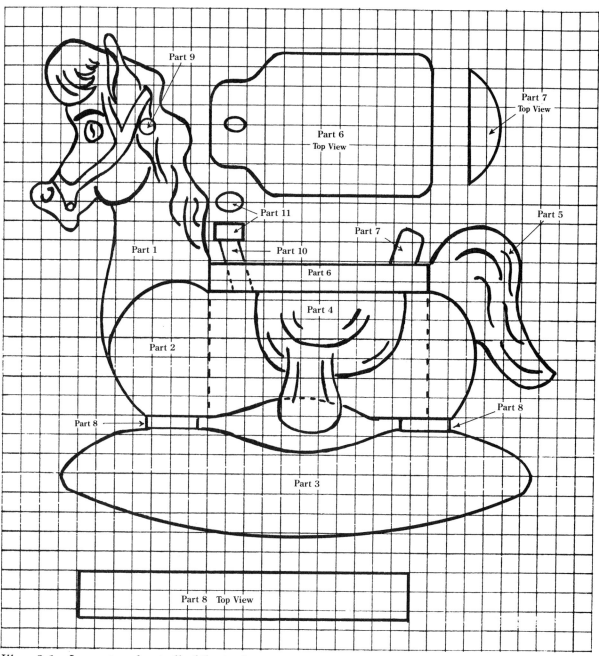

Illus. 2.1   Lay out and cut all of the parts.

If you have a youngster in your household who has a fancy for horses or wants to try their hand at taming the wild west, they are sure to get a real kick out of this prize-winning palomino. The sturdy construction and timeless attraction of this project makes it one that your young cowpoke will be able to pass on to future generations of ranch hands.

Safety is a serious consideration in the design of all of our toys and the rocking horse is no exception. It has a low center of gravity and a wide rocking foundation which makes accidental turnover highly unlikely. Its design also eliminates sharp corners and protrusions.

This rocking horse can be constructed in a couple of afternoons, excluding the final varnishing, so it should make a nice weekend project.

Materials List

2" × 8" (5.08 cm × 20 cm)
  Douglas fir (dry) . . . . 12 feet (3.66 meters)
2" × 12" (5.08 cm × 30.5 cm) Douglas fir (dry) . . . . . 24" (61 cm)
1" × 3" (2.54 cm × 7.62 cm) hardwood such as ash or maple . . . . 3 feet (1 meter)
1" (2.54 cm) dowel . . . . 15" (38 cm)
Carriage bolts:
  ¼" × 4¾" (6.35 mm × 12 cm) 4
  ¼" × 5" (6.35 mm × 12.7 cm) 8
  ¼" × 3¼" (6.35 mm × 8.25 cm) 4
¼" (6.35 mm) flat washers . . 16
¼" (6.35 mm) machine nuts, 12
¼" (6.35 mm) acorn nuts . . . 4

1½" (3.81 cm) woodscrews,
  No. 10 flathead 10
Nontoxic clear varnish . . . . . . 1 pint
Nontoxic paint for the facial features and hairline: White, brown, black and blue in small amounts

Cutting List

Part 1 . . . Head . . . . Make 1
Part 2 . . . Body . . . . Make 2
Part 3 . . . Rocker . . . . Make 2
Part 4 . . . Side of Saddle . . . . Make 2
Part 5 . . . Tail . . . . Make 1
Part 6 . . . Saddle Seat . . . . Make 1
Part 7 . . . Saddle Back . . . . Make 1
Part 8 . . . Rocker Spanner . . . . Make 2
Part 9* . . . Handle . . . . Make 1
Part 10**. Stem of Saddle Horn . . . Make 1
Part 11† . . Top of Saddle Horn . . . . Make 1

*Part 9 is a 1" × 12" (2.54 cm × 30.5 cm) length of dowel.
**One end is cut at a 15° angle.
†Part 11 is ¾" (19 mm) material cut into a ½" ellipse.

Instructions

LAYOUT

1. Lay out all parts (Illus. 2.1 and 2.2) on 2" × 8" (5.08 cm × 20 cm) material with the exception of the head (Part 1), two rocker spanners (Part 8), and Parts 9, 10 and 11 as directed in the cutting list.
2. Lay out the head (Part 1) on 2" × 12" (5.08 cm × 30.5 cm) material.
3. Lay out the rocker spanners (Part 8) on 1" × 3" (2.54 cm × 7.62 cm) hardwood material.
4. Cut out all the rest of the parts.
5. Sand all of these parts well.

FINISHING EDGES

6. Using a ½″ (12.7 mm) corner-round router bit, router the following edges to a ½″ (12.7 mm) radius:

   Part 4 . . . Entire outside perimeter except top edge

   Part 6 . . . Entire perimeter of top side

   Part 7 . . . Rounded top side on both edges

   Part 8 . . . Entire perimeter on top side

7. Using a ¼″ (6.35 mm) corner-round router bit, router the following edges to a ¼″ (6.35 mm) radius:

   Part 2 . . . Entire outside perimeter

   Part 3 . . . Entire perimeter of both sides

   Parts 1 and 5 . . . All edges of both sides that extend above the body assembly

   NOTE: Although these radiused edges improve the finished appearance of the hobby horse, the primary purpose is to eliminate sharp corners. With safety in mind, these steps should not be overlooked.

ASSEMBLY

8. Locate and drill the two holes on Part 1. The one hole is for the bridle to pass through. It is a ⅜″ (9.5 mm)-diameter hole located near the horse's mouth. The other hole is for mounting the handle. It is a 1″ (2.54 cm)-diameter hole near the back of the horse's head (Illus. 2.3).

9. Notice that the head (Part 1), the tail (Part 5) and the sides of the saddle (Part 4) have detail marks to add character and style to the horse's appearance. (Illus. 2.3 and 2.4). These marks should be drawn in at this time.

   NOTE: Parts 1 and 5 will have these marks on both sides.

10. The detail marks should be painted. The hair lines on Parts 1 and 5 are to be painted black, as are the ear outline, the nose, the

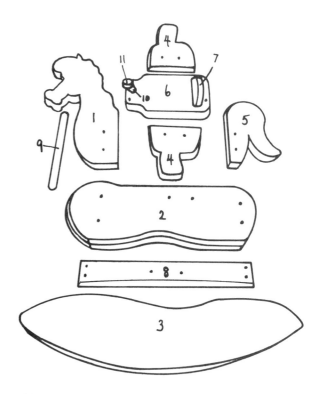

Illus. 2.2   Rocking Horse parts.

Illus. 2.3   Drill holes in the horse's head for the handle and bridle. Paint the facial features on.

Illus. 2.4 Paint the details on the saddle sides. Use carriage bolts for assembly.

jawbone, the eye outline and the eyebrow. The head harness on Part 1 and the detail saddle marks on Part 4 may be painted brown. The eyes are to be painted white with blue marks.

11. To assemble the rocker assembly, ⁹⁄₃₂″ (7.14 mm)-diameter holes should be drilled through the end of the rocker spanners (Part 8) and all the way through the rockers from the top to the bottom. Then these holes should be countersunk back up from the bottom to a diameter of ¾″ (19 mm) and to a depth of 1½″ (3.81 cm). Refer to Illus. 2.5. Use ¼″ × 5″ (6.35 mm × 12.7 cm) carriage bolts with ¼″ (6.35 mm) flat washers and nuts to secure this assembly together (Illus. 2.6).

12. Locate and secure the saddle sides (Part 4) to the two body parts (Part B) as shown in Illus. 2.2 and 2.4. Secure the parts together by drilling two ⁹⁄₃₂″ (7.14 mm)-diameter holes and using ¼″ × 3¼″ (6.35 mm × 8.25 cm) carriage bolts and ¼″ (6.35 mm) flat washers and nuts.

13. The two body parts (Part 2), the head (Part 1) and tail (Part 5) are to be assembled with four ¼″ × 4¾″ (6.35 mm × 12 cm) carriage bolts; two installed in ⁹⁄₃₂″ (7.14 mm) holes drilled through the forward end of the body (Part 2) and the head (Part 1) and two more in ⁹⁄₃₂″ (7.14 mm) holes toward the

rear of the body for the tail (Part 5, Illus. 2.8). Secure the bolts in place with ¼″ (6.35 mm) flat washers and acorn nuts. The acorn nuts are called for at this point for safety purposes because both ends of the carriage bolts are exposed.

14. Center the horse's body assembly over the rocker assembly and secure from the bottom side with four 1½″ (3.81 cm) wood screws.
NOTE: Adjust the weight slightly to the front or rear to allow the completed unit to set level.

15. Drill the 1″ (2.54 cm) hole in the saddle seat (Part 6) at a 15° angle to a depth of 1″ (2.54 cm).

16. Using carpenter's glue, install Part 10 in this hole (Illus. 2.7).
NOTE: Be sure to install so that the end cut at a 15° angle is exposed and turned so as to be parallel with the top of the seat.

17. Secure Part 11 to the top of this dowel using carpenter's glue and 1½″ (3.81 cm) finishing nails. Predrill these nail holes to prevent splitting and counterset the nails. Fill the nail holes with wood putty and sand smooth when putty is dry.

18. The saddle back (Part 7) can be secured to the saddle seat with 1½″ (3.81 cm) No. 10

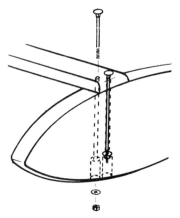

Illus. 2.5 Detail of rocker assembly.

Illus. 2.6   The rocker assembly is secured together with carriage bolts.

Illus. 2.7   Saddle assembly.

woodscrews installed from the bottom of the seat (Illus. 2.7).

19. Secure the saddle assembly to the horse assembly with 1½″ (3.81 cm) No. 10 flathead woodscrews installed directly from the top of the saddle seat. Countersink these screw heads to a depth of ¹⁄₁₆″ (1.6 mm) for safety purposes.

20. Center the handle through the 1″ (2.54 cm) hole in the back of the head (Part 1) and secure in place with two 1½″ (3.81 cm)

flathead woodscrews installed through the back edge of the head and countersunk to a depth of ¹⁄₁₆″ (1.6 mm) for safety (Illus. 2.9).

21. The entire assembly can be varnished with several coats of clear varnish.

Your classic Rocking Horse is now complete and ready for its first ride across the open range.

Illus. 2.8   Assemble the body parts together with carriage bolts.

Illus. 2.9   Install handle with flathead woodscrews.

Chapter 3
Wheels for the Rolling Stock

A toy builder will not be at work for very long before realizing a serious need for realistic-looking wheels. Wheels are fairly readily available from wooden parts-supply houses, wooden toy pattern companies are even well-outfitted building supply stores. These wheels are all manufactured by machines and although they are very well done, sometimes they just don't look quite right, especially on a toy that has a fairly high degree of detail and realism.

You can usually obtain a more desirable, realistic-looking wheel by making your own. Making wheels, however, is somewhat time consuming, so it really comes to a toss-up of time versus desired appearance. Then there are also the times when the particular toy in question looks just fine with the commercially available wheels and there is no need to spend the extra time.

Let us look at how to make the wheels for the racing cars and fire truck that appear in the next chapter. This way you'll have a feel for how to make wheels for yourself and then you can choose what best suits your needs.

The first thing that you should do is to decide what size wheel you need. Give yourself a range such as 1½″ to 1¾″ (3.81 cm to 4.45 cm) diameter if you can. Your finished wheel diameter will be cut with a hole saw and an exact size may not always be possible. In this case, a 1¾″ (4.45 cm) hole saw can be used and give a finished wheel

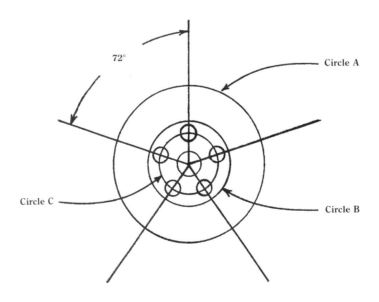

Illus. 3.1   Wheel diagram.

diameter of 1⅝″ (4.13 cm). This is within your size range and will work out fine for each of the toys that they are made for.

Next, of course, you must consider what wheels on racing cars often look like. They usually are mag-type wheels with about five holes around the center hub. Racing tires are normally very wide and overhang the wheel somewhat. The tire width will be determined by the thickness of the stock from which these parts will be cut. In our case, standard ¹³⁄₁₆″ (20.6 mm) flat stock maple will work out perfectly. In the future, if you have an application which requires wider wheels you can simply use thicker stock, or rip down to thinner stock for narrower wheels.

Maple, by the way, is the recommended material to use for wheels because it has a great deal of strength even when ripped to narrow thicknesses. The construction process alone for these wheels puts them under quite a torture test, not to mention what they will be subjected to during the "Living Room 500"; one pit stop and you've lost the race.

To actually lay out the wheel for construction, draw a 1⅝″ (4.13 cm)-diameter circle on the material to be used. This is shown on Illus. 3.1 as Circle A and represents the finished diameter of the completed wheel and tire.

Now draw a ⅞″ (22.2 mm)-diameter circle inside the larger one (Circle B on Illus. 4-A). This will be the diameter of the hubcap inside the tire.

Once more, now, draw a ⅝″ (1.6 cm)-diameter circle centered inside the others, which is Circle C (Illus. 3.1 and 3.2).

To locate the position of the five small mag-wheel holes, draw five straight lines out from the center of the circle. These lines will be 72° apart as shown in Illus. 3.1. Each point where

Illus. 3.2   Layout of toy wheel on ¾″ (1.9 cm) hardwood stock.

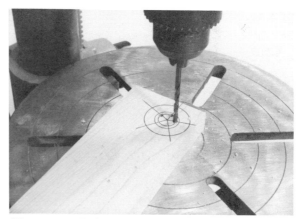

Illus. 3.3   Drill out the five mag-wheel holes.

Illus. 3.4   Drill the center (wheel portion) to a depth of ⅛″ (3.18 mm).

Illus. 3.5   Use a hole saw to relieve the wheel from the flat stock.

Illus. 3.6   Use a drill press as a mini-lathe to shape the finished wheel.

one of these lines and Circle C intersect is a drilling center mark for one of the small holes. Centerpunch these marks and the center of the wheel.

Maple is a very hard wood and drilling it is fairly difficult if you do not first centerpunch the drilling locations to minimize drill drift.

Now, with your drill press fitted with a ³⁄₁₆″ (4.75 mm) drill bit, simply drill out each of the mag-wheel holes (Illus. 3.3).

Next, use a ⅞″ (22.2 mm) center bore drill bit and drill the wheel portion of the assembly to a depth of approximately ⅛″ (3.18 mm) as shown in Illus. 3.4.

Last of all, you can now use the 1¾″ (4.45 cm) hole saw to relieve the entire wheel from the flat stock. Using the hole saw from both sides and cutting only a portion of the way through gives a cleaner finished product (Illus. 3.5).

To debur and shape the wheel, you can use your drill press as sort of a mini lathe. Drill out the center hole in the wheel to ¼″ (6.35 mm) so that it will later fit a ¼″ (6.35 mm) dowel axle. Now take a ¼″ (6.35 mm) bolt about 3 or 4 inches (6.35 cm to 10 cm) long and cut off the head with a hack saw. Then fit the wooden

Illus. 3.7   A small backsaw can be used to make the tire tread.

Illus. 3.8   Mark the next wheel with hole saw.

Illus. 3.9   Use original wheel as a drilling template.

Illus. 3.10   Duplicate the first wheel several times simultaneously.

wheel on the other end (the threaded end) and secure it between two ¼″ (6.35 mm) nuts.

Chuck the bolt into the drill press. Set the press to rotate at a medium speed and use a wood rasp and sandpaper to clean up and bring the wheel to the desired shape (Illus. 3.6).

Of course, no self-respecting race-car tire would ever show its face without a proper tread. So while still chucked up in the drill press, take a small back saw and cut five or six marks into the outer circumference of this new wheel (Illus. 3.7).

Fit the drill press once again with the hole saw and mark another wheel by drilling slightly into the flat stock (Illus. 3.8). Then drill out the

center hole to ¼″ (6.35 mm) and use a ¼″ (6.35 mm) dowel about 2″ (5.08 cm) long to pin the finished wheel to the flat stock, making it a template for drilling the ³⁄₁₆″ (4.75 mm) mag-wheel holes (Illus. 3.9). After the first ³⁄₁₆″ (4.75 mm) hole is drilled, another dowel of ³⁄₁₆″ (4.75 mm) diameter can be used to prevent the template wheel from spinning during the five drilling operations.

Actually, the duplication of the first wheel can be done a number of times simultaneously (Illus. 3.10), creating enough wheels for all the race car projects you might have in mind. You may even want to stock-pile a few if you think that the wheel design will work out for other toys.

Chapter 4
The Racing Circuit

You'll have a great time with these little racing machines. As they begin to take shape in your hands, you'll almost be able to hear the roar of those high performance racing engines, smell the exhaust of alcohol-mixed fuel, and feel the tremendous speeds implied by the sleek shapes and aerodynamic designs.

The Formula 9 is patterned after the super-fast, modern-day "Indy" racers, complete with airfoil spoilers for stability on high-speed straightaways, and a helmeted driver nestled deep into the cockpit.

The Grand Prix Racer, aside from wheels and axles, has only three parts: The simplicity of its design is a paradox to its realistic appearance

and the captivating effect it has on the younger set.

No racing-circuit manager would allow the green flag to fly until he was assured that all safety and fire crews were standing by in complete readiness. The Little Red Fire Engine is another simple toy to build, but it has the detail needed to make it a front-runner in popularity with the youngsters.

These toys are excellent projects for the young toy builder. They generate an excitement of their own, even before the final steps of construction. For safety's sake, be sure to provide plenty of supervision, especially when the use of power tools is required.

Formula 9

Materials List

Hardwood stock (birch, maple, alder, etc.) .... *1½" × 1¾" × 10" (3.81 cm × 4.45 cm × 25.4 cm)*

¾" (19 mm) hardwood stock, *4" or 5" square (10.16 cm × 12.7 cm square)*

¼" (6.35 mm) hardwood dowel .... *18" (45 cm)*

½" (12.7 mm) hardwood dowel .... *6" (15 cm)*

Illus. 4.1

⅛″ (3.18 mm) hardwood
  dowel .... 3″ (7.62 cm)
Carpenter's glue .... small container
1¾″ (4.45 cm) finishing nails, small box
1½″ to 1¾″ (3.81 cm to 4.45
  cm) diameter hardwood toy
  wheels 4
Nontoxic paint: two or three colors in small
containers

Cutting List

Part 1 ... Race Car Body .... Make 1
Part 2 ... Rear Spoiler Support ... Make 2
Part 3 ... Rear Spoiler .... Make 1
Part 4 ... Exhaust Pipe .... Make 2
Part 5 ... Forward Spoiler .... Make 2

Instructions

LAYOUT

1. Lay out the profile shape and mark the three drilling locations for the race-car body (Part 1) on a piece of hardwood material that has a thickness of 1½″ (3.81 cm) and a minimum width of 1¾″ (4.45 cm) (Illus. 4.2).

2. Beginning with a piece of ¾″ (19 mm) hardwood material approximately 4″ × 5″ (10.16 cm × 12.7 cm) in size, rip a ¼″ (6.35 mm) slab from it.

3. Lay out Parts 2, 3 (Illus. 4.3) and 5 (Illus. 4.4) on this piece of ¼″ (6.35 mm) material. You will need two each of Parts 2 and 5.

4. With the use of a bandsaw, cut each of Parts 1, 2, 3, and 5 to shape.

5. Drill the three holes marked in Illus. 4.2 completely through Part 1. A drill press should be used for best results.

BODY

6. Refer to the area marked Section A on Illus. 4.2. This is a rear view of the engine cowling, or the portion of the race-car body immediately behind the driver's head. As shown in this drawing, each side of this engine cowling should now be cut to a 45° angle (Illus. 4.2 and 4.6).

7. In the Section A drawing you will also notice two drilling location marks. Mark these locations and drill two ¼″ (6.35 mm)-diameter holes to a depth of ½″ (12.7 mm). These holes are the mounting holes for the two exhaust pipes (Part 4).
   NOTE: Drill carefully, because there is very little clearance to the outside edge of the engine cowling.

8. Sand the race car body (Part 1) and radius the edges to create a more aerodynamic effect.

9. Using ¼″ (6.35 mm) hardwood dowel stock, measure and cut the two exhaust pipes (Part 4). Sand these parts well.

10. Use carpenter's glue to secure the two exhaust pipes (Part 4) into the two ¼″ (6.35 mm) holes at the rear of the engine cowling.
    NOTE: Be sure that these two parts extend equally from the engine cowling and that the 30° angle is properly aligned on each (Illus. 4.6).

11. Now sand and shape Parts 2, 3 and 5 as shown in Illus. 4.3 and 4.4.

SPOILER ASSEMBLY

12. Secure the rear spoiler assembly (Parts 2 and 3) into place with carpenter's glue just behind the engine cowling (Illus. 4.1).

13. After the glue has set, drill two ¹⁄₁₆″ (1.6 mm)-diameter holes through Part 3 and each Part 2 into the car body as shown in Illus. 4.3.

14. Drive a 1¾″ (4.45 cm) finishing nail into each of these holes to give extra strength to

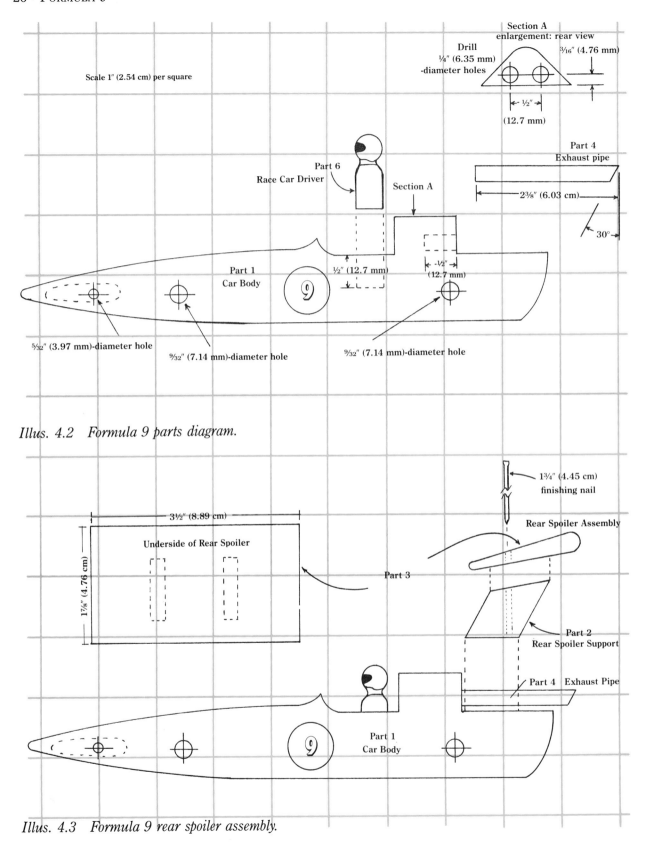

Scale 1″ (2.54 cm) per square

Section A
enlargement: rear view

Drill
¼″ (6.35 mm)
-diameter holes

³⁄₁₆″ (4.76 mm)

½″
(12.7 mm)

Part 4
Exhaust pipe

2³⁄₈″ (6.03 cm)

30°

Part 6
Race Car Driver

Section A

Part 1
Car Body

9

½″ (12.7 mm)

½″
(12.7 mm)

⁵⁄₃₂″ (3.97 mm)-diameter hole

⁹⁄₃₂″ (7.14 mm)-diameter hole

⁹⁄₃₂″ (7.14 mm)-diameter hole

Illus. 4.2   Formula 9 parts diagram.

1¾″ (4.45 cm)
finishing nail

Rear Spoiler Assembly

3½″ (8.89 cm)

Underside of Rear Spoiler

1⁷⁄₈″ (4.76 cm)

Part 3

Part 2
Rear Spoiler Support

Part 4   Exhaust Pipe

9

Part 1
Car Body

Illus. 4.3   Formula 9 rear spoiler assembly.

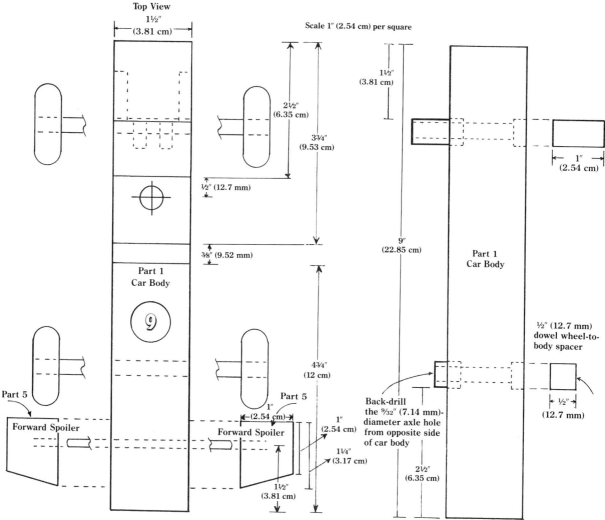

Illus. 4.4 *Top view of Formula 9 parts.*

Illus. 4.5 *Detail of axle assembly.*

this rear spoiler installation (Illus. 4.3). Set these nails, fill the holes and sand smooth.

15. Drill a ⅛″ (3.18 mm)-diameter hole into the edge of each forward spoiler (Part 5) as indicated in Illus. 4.4. Drill these holes to a depth of ½″ (12.7 mm).

16. Cut a section of ⅛″ (3.18 mm) hardwood dowel to a length of 2⅜″ (6 cm).

17. Use carpenter's glue and this ⅛″ (3.18 mm) dowel section to install and secure the forward spoilers (Part 5) as indicated in Illus. 4.1 and 4.4.

NOTE: Be sure that each spoiler is aligned with the other and the car body *before* the glue sets.

WHEELS AND DRIVER

18. Illus. 4.5 shows the installation of the wheel-to-body spacers. These spacers are made from ½″ (12.7 mm) dowel stock. Cut four wheel-to-body spacers at this time. Two of these spacers will be 1″ (2.54 cm) long: these are the rear wheel-to-body

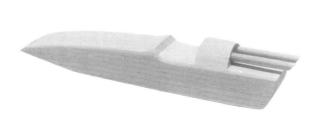

Illus. 4.6   Formula 9 body assembly.

Illus. 4.7   Shape the driver in a drill press.

spacers. The front spacers are to be ½″ (12.7 mm) long.

19. Using a ½″ (1.27 cm) drill bit, countersink each side of both axle holes to a depth of ¼″ (6.35 mm).

20. Use carpenter's glue to install the wheel-to-body spacers into one side of the car body. Install both the rear and front spacer on one side only.

21. After the glue has set, back drill the 9/32″ (7.14 mm)-diameter axle hole through the wheel-to-body spacer from the other side of the race car body (Illus. 4.4).

22. Repeat this installation and drilling process for the spacers on the other side.

23. Locate and drill the ½″ (12.7 mm)-diameter hole to a depth of ½″ (1.27 cm) into the center of the cockpit area for the driver's hole (Illus. 4.3).

24. Chuck a short section of ½″ (12.7 mm) hardwood dowel into a drill press.

25. Using a wood rasp and sandpaper, shape the race car driver (Part 6) as indicated in Illus. 4.2 and 4.7 while the drill press is turning at a medium speed.

26. After the driver (Part 6) is shaped, cut it to a length of 1¼″ (3.18 cm).

NOTE: You will probably want to delay gluing the driver into the cockpit until after it is painted.

27. The axles are to be cut from ¼″ (6.35 mm) dowel stock. The exact length of the axles will be determined by the type of wheels you have chosen to use. If you use the wheels described in Chapter 4, the front axle will have a length of 3¼″ (8.25 cm) and the rear axle will be 4¼″ (10.8 cm) long.

28. The installation of the wheels should be delayed until the painting process has been completed.

29. Using nontoxic paints of your color choice, paint the entire project.

30. Complete the assembly after painting by gluing the driver into the cockpit and securing the wheels to the axles with glue. Be careful not to allow any glue to get into the axle hole of the wheel-to-body spacers and cause binding of the axle operation.

Your Formula 9 racing car is now complete and ready to begin the time trials for the big race. Handle it well and it will be a winner for you.

Grand Prix Racer

Materials List

Hardwood stock . . . . *2¼″ × 2½″ ×*
10″ (5.72 cm ×
6.35 cm ×
25.4 cm)

¾″ (19 mm) hardwood stock, *4″ × 10″*
(10.16 cm ×
25.4 cm)

¼″ (6.35 mm) hardwood
dowel . . . . *10″ (25.4 cm)*

1¾″ (4.45 cm) finishing nails, small box

Carpenter's glue . . . . *small container*

1½″ to 1⅝″ (3.81 cm to 4.13
cm)-diameter hardwood toy
wheels *4*

Nontoxic paints: two or three colors in small
containers

Cutting List

Part 1 . . . *Body Center Section* . . . *Make 1*
Part 2 . . . *Body Side Section* . . . . . *Make 2*

Instructions

LAYOUT

1. Use a block of hardwood stock 2¼″ × 2½″ × 10″ (5.72 cm × 6.35 cm × 25.4 cm). This hardwood block can be fabricated by laminating several thinner pieces of wood together (Illus. 4.11). Lay out the race car body center section (Part 1) in profile on the 2¼″ (5.72 cm) side (Illus. 4.9). Also locate and mark the two drilling locations for the axle holes.
2. Lay out the race-car side (Part 2) on the ¾″ (19 mm) stock. You will need two of these.

Illus. 4.8

3. Using a bandsaw, cut these three pieces to shape (Illus. 4.9, 4.10 and 4.12).
4. Drill the axle holes in the center section (Part 1) that are shown in Illus. 4.9. Use a drill press for best results, and drill completely through the part.
5. Sand the parts well. Radius the outsides of the side sections, the edge of the cockpit canopy section and the inside of the front fenders to create a sleek, aerodynamic effect.

ASSEMBLY

6. Align and secure the two side sections to each side of the center section with carpenter's glue and 1¾″ (4.45 cm) finishing nails. Set these nails, fill the holes and sand smooth.
7. Use nontoxic paints of your color choice and paint the race car body at this time.
8. The length of the axles will depend upon the particular wheels that you choose for this project. If you use the wheels described in Chapter 3, both axles will be 3¾″ (9.52 cm) long. Cut these axles from ¼″ (6.35 mm) hardwood dowel stock.

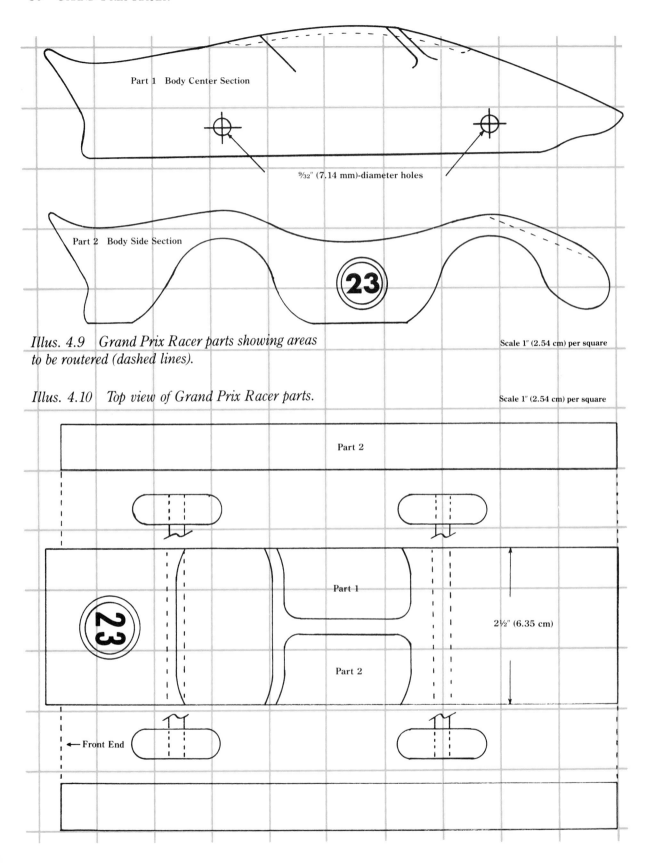

Part 1   Body Center Section

⁹⁄₃₂″ (7.14 mm)-diameter holes

Part 2   Body Side Section

23

Illus. 4.9   Grand Prix Racer parts showing areas to be routered (dashed lines).

Scale 1″ (2.54 cm) per square

Illus. 4.10   Top view of Grand Prix Racer parts.

Scale 1″ (2.54 cm) per square

Part 2

23

Part 1

2½″ (6.35 cm)

Part 2

← Front End

Illus. 4.11   Fabricate the block needed for the race car body by laminating several thinner pieces together.

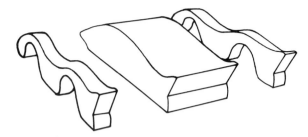

Illus. 4.12   Use a bandsaw to cut these three pieces to shape.

9. Paint the wheels black with a color-coordinated center hub.
10. Install the wheels by gluing them to the ¼" (6.35 mm) axles. Remember to keep the glue away from the axle holes of the race car itself so that free spinning axles will be maintained.

Your Grand Prix Racer is now complete. You will find that properly tuned, she will reach straightaway speeds in excess of 270 mph (435 kph) and will handle hairpin corners with no problem whatsoever. A good driver should have no trouble in taking the checkered flag in her.

Little Red Fire Engine

Materials List

Hardwood stock . . . . *1¾" × 3½" × 8" (4.45 cm × 8.9 cm × 20 cm)*

Hardwood stock . . . . *¾" × 3½" × 16" (19 mm × 8.9 cm × 40.6 cm)*

⁷⁄₁₆" (11.1 mm) hardwood dowel . . . . *2" (5.08 cm)*

¼" (6.35 mm) hardwood dowel . . . . *30" (76 cm)*

⅛" (3.18 mm) hardwood dowel . . . . *18" (45.7 cm)*

1½" to 1¾ (3.81 cm to 4.45 cm)-diameter hardwood toy wheels *4*

Illus. 4.13

Carpenter's glue . . . . *small container*
1¾" (4.45 cm) finishing nails, small box
Nontoxic paint: small containers in red, yellow, black, white and silver

Cutting List

Part 1 . . . Body Center . . . . *Make 1*
Part 2 . . . Body Side . . . . *Make 2*

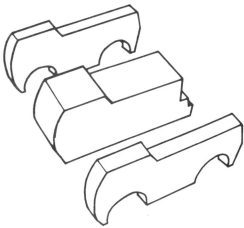

Illus. 4.14   Use a bandsaw to cut the fire engine parts to shape.

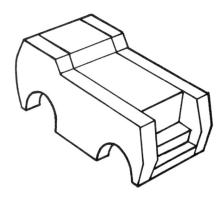

Illus. 4.15   Secure these parts together.

Instructions

LAYOUT

1. Lay out the center section of the fire engine body (Part 1) on a 1¾″ × 3½″ × 8″ (4.45 cm × 8.9 cm × 20 cm) piece of hardwood stock (Illus. 4.16 and 4.18). Also mark the axle hole drilling locations.
2. Lay out the body side sections (Part 2) on ¾″ × 3½″ × 16″ (19 mm × 8.9 cm × 40.5 cm) material. You will need two of these (Illus. 4.17 and 4.18).
3. Use a bandsaw and cut these three parts to shape (Illus. 4.14).

ASSEMBLY

4. Drill the ⁹⁄₃₂″ (7.14 mm) axle holes in Part 1 as shown in Illus. 4.16. For best results, a drill press should be used for this operation if one is available.
5. Align and secure Part 1 and the two Part 2's together with carpenter's glue and 1¾″ (4.45 cm) finishing nails. Set these nails, fill the holes and sand to a smooth finish (Illus. 4.15).
6. Mark the location of the emergency lights on top of the truck cab (Illus. 4.18).

7. Use a ⁷⁄₁₆″ (11.1 mm) drill and drill these two holes to a depth of ½″ (1.27 cm).
8. Cut two dowel sections from ⁷⁄₁₆″ (11.1 mm) dowel stock to a length of ⅞″ (22.2 mm) and sand these parts well.
9. Use carpenter's glue to secure these parts into the holes on the top of the truck cab. NOTE: Be sure that each of the dowels extends the same amount from the cab top.

PAINTING

10. Paint the truck body bright red with a white window area.
    NOTE: Slash the white windows with silver paint to create the effect of glass.
11. Fabricate the ladder, fire extinguisher and ax on each side of the fire engine by using ¼″ (6.35 mm) and ⅛″ (3.18 mm) dowel stock and gluing the parts together and to the side of the fire engine (Illus. 4.17).
12. The parts should be painted as follows: ladder, yellow; extinguisher, red with silver and black trim; ax, yellow handle, silver blade.
13. The axle length will be determined by the particular wheel that you choose to install

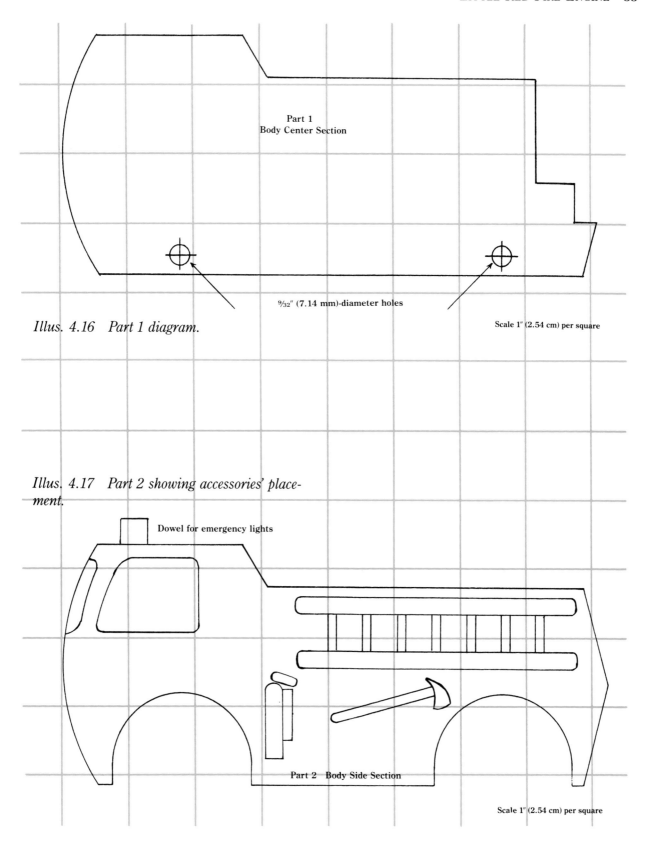

Part 1
Body Center Section

9/32″ (7.14 mm)-diameter holes

Illus. 4.16   Part 1 diagram.

Scale 1″ (2.54 cm) per square

*Illus. 4.17   Part 2 showing accessories' place-
ment.*

Dowel for emergency lights

Part 2   Body Side Section

Scale 1″ (2.54 cm) per square

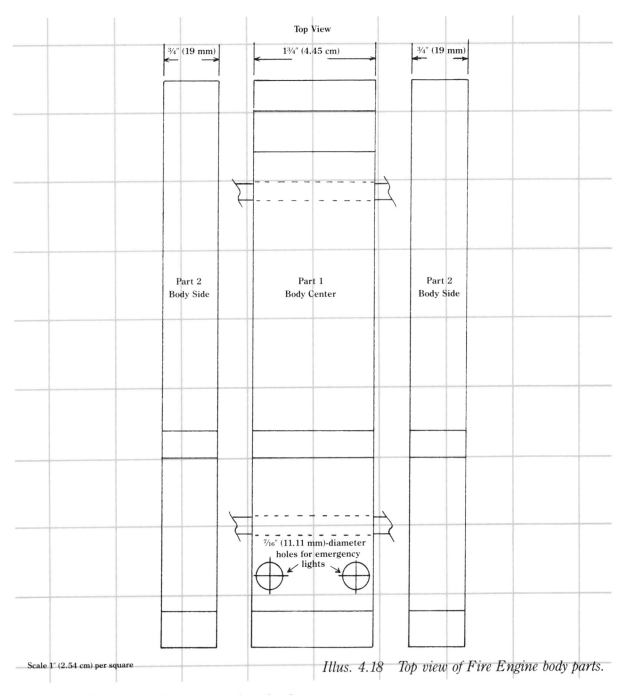

Top View

¾″ (19 mm)   1¾″ (4.45 cm)   ¾″ (19 mm)

Part 2
Body Side

Part 1
Body Center

Part 2
Body Side

⁷⁄₁₆″ (11.11 mm)-diameter
holes for emergency
lights

Scale 1″ (2.54 cm) per square

Illus. 4.18   Top view of Fire Engine body parts.

on your fire engine. If you select the wheels discussed in Chapter 4, then the length of the axles will be 3″ (7.62 cm).

14. Paint the wheels black and trim the center hub either silver or red.

15. Install the wheels by gluing them to the ¼″ (6.35 mm) dowel axles. Do not allow the glue to get into the revolving area of the axles and the truck body.

This Little Red Fire Engine is now ready for action to save the racing drivers and to protect life and limb from the harmful effect of fire out of control.

Chapter 5
Air-Sea Rescue

It is not always necessary to create highly realistic, extremely detailed toys for children. Oftentimes simplicity in the toy's design enhances its attraction to the child. The airplanes in this chapter are toys in this category. Their designs are quite simple with relatively few parts. They are quick and easy to build, and yet their popularity with children is unequaled.

I have chosen to call this type of toy "the profile toy," for it takes virtually all of its character when viewed from the profile or side view. This design concept has unlimited possibilities because almost everything around us can be reduced to a profile and simplified to a few basic shapes. As you build these toys and become familiar with this style of design, you might try a couple of profile designs of your own. I bet you'll do a great job and I know you'll have a lot of fun in the process.

The air-sea rescue squadron is composed of three different airplanes. The Bush Plane is designed to patrol wilderness areas for wandering fishermen and hikers. It is fitted with pontoon landing-gear to facilitate rescues from mountain lake landing areas. It is made up of only six parts and makes a wonderful afternoon project. The Rescue Helicopter is used along the coastline for monitoring small craft safety and to keep an eye on beachfront activities. It, too, is equipped with pontoons for rescue operations in the choppy waters just off shore. Consisting of only four parts, this one can be done in a couple of hours.

For long-range reconnaissance operations over the high seas, the Navy Sea Plane is just the ticket. Two powerful engines allow hours of nonstop flight while the three-man crew search the sea below for signs of life. Sensitive onboard radar equipment makes this search and rescue aircraft even more effective. It is specifically designed for sea landings with a boat-shaped fuselage and wing-mounted pontoons. Its engines and tail section are mounted high above the salt spray to assure trouble-free performance. Last, but by no means least, it has the capacity to carry 15–20 survivors to safety and medical attention. This little aircraft should take one afternoon to construct, and offers great fun for the builder *and* the pilot.

Bush Plane

Materials List

¾" (19 mm) hardwood stock, 5" × 20" (12.7 cm × 50 cm)

Carpenter's glue . . . . small container
1¾" (4.45 cm) finishing nails, small box
No. 6 × 1" (2.54 cm)
*   roundhead woodscrew 1*
No. 6 Flat washer 1
Nontoxic paint: colors of your choice in small containers

Illus. 5.1

Cutting List

Part 1 ... Fuselage . . . . Make 1
Part 2 ... Pontoon . . . . Make 2
Part 3 ... Wing . . . . Make 1
Part 4 ... Tail . . . . Make 1
Part 5 ... Propeller . . . . Make 1

Instructions

LAYOUT

1. Lay out the fuselage (Part 1) and two pontoons (Part 2) on the ¾" (19 mm) material stock (Illus. 5.2 and 5.4).

2. Cut these parts to shape, sand well and set them aside.

3. The wing, tail and propeller (Parts 3, 4, and 5) are each to be cut from stock that is thinner than the ¾" (19 mm) material called for. Therefore, this material must be ripped to the thickness indicated in Illus. 5.3.

4. Lay out Parts 3, 4, and 5 (Illus. 5.3) on the material prepared in Step 3 and cut each part to shape. Sand these parts well and prepare them for assembly.

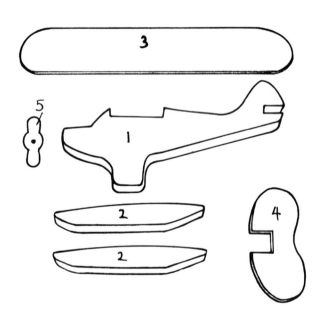

Illus. 5.2 Lay out and cut the parts for the Bush Plane.

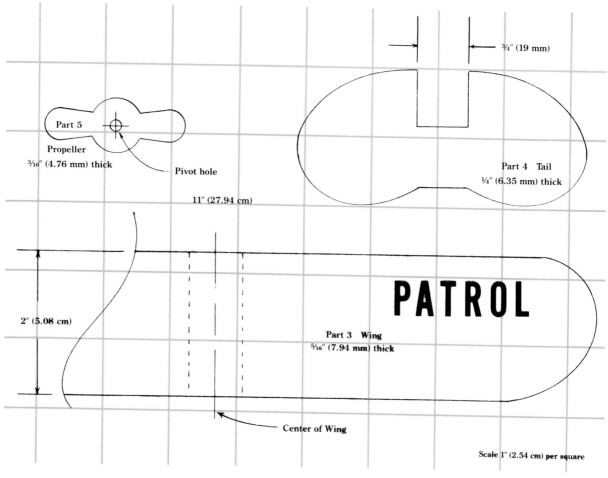

Illus. 5.3   Bush Plane parts detail.

ASSEMBLY

5. Fit the wing (Part 3) and the tail (Part 4) into the respective notches in the fuselage (Part 1) to be sure of proper fit. Make any necessary adjustments to these notches with a wood rasp and sandpaper to facilitate a good fit for each of these parts.

6. Now assemble Parts 1, 2, 3, and 4 as indicated on Illus. 5.1 and 5.4. Use carpenter's glue and 1¾″ (4.45 cm) finishing nails. Set the nails, fill the nail holes and sand smooth. NOTE: Be sure both pontoons (Part 2) are properly aligned so the airplane will stand correctly and not rock.

7. Drill a small pilot hole into the center of the nose of the fuselage where the propeller will be mounted.

8. Drill a hole through the center of the propeller (Part 5). This hole should be slightly larger than the diameter of the No. 6 screw to be used, so that the propeller will spin freely.

9. Install the propeller (Part 5) to the nose of the fuselage (Part 6) by use of the No. 6 × 1″ (2.54 cm) roundhead woodscrew. Place the small flat washer between the propeller and the fuselage. This acts as a bearing surface and allows the propeller to operate

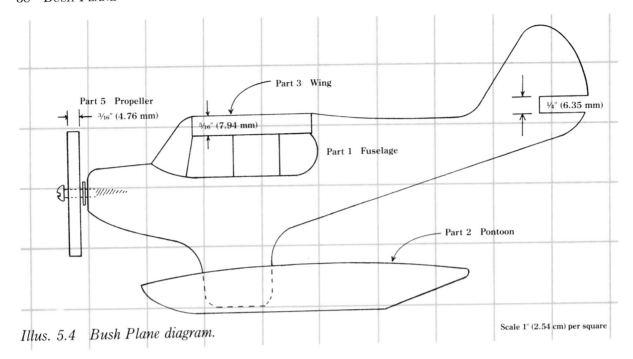

Illus. 5.4 Bush Plane diagram.

more freely. Tighten the screw enough to prevent the propeller from wobbling, but not so tight as to prevent it from spinning freely.

10. After the propeller has been installed and correctly adjusted it should be removed again for the painting operation.

11. Use nontoxic paints of your color choice and paint the entire project. The windshield design can be painted white and slashed with silver streaks to give the appearance of glass. This toy also looks attractive if the windshield and wing markings are done with a wood-burning set, and then the entire project is finished in a clear varnish.

12. Reinstall the propeller after the painting process is finished.

Your Bush Plane is now ready for its first flight into the back country.

Rescue Helicopter

Materials List

¾″ (19 mm) hardwood stock,   3″ × 14″ (7.6 cm × 35.6 cm)

Carpenter's glue . . . . small container
1¾″ (4.45 cm) finishing nails, small box
No. 6 × 1″ (2.54 cm)
  roundhead woodscrew 1
No. 6 flat washer 1
Nontoxic paint: colors of your choice in small containers

Illus. 5.5

Cutting List

Part 1 . . . Fuselage . . . . Make 1
Part 2 . . . Pontoon/Fuel Tank . . . . . Make 2
Part 3 . . . Rotor . . . . Make 1

Instructions

LAYOUT

1. Lay out the fuselage (Part 1) and two pontoon/fuel tank assemblies (Part 2) on ¾″ (19 mm) material and cut to shape according to Illus. 5.6 and 5.7. Sand these pieces well to prepare them for assembly.

ASSEMBLY

2. Assemble Parts 1 and 2 as shown in Illus. 5.5 and 5.7. Be sure of proper alignment of pontoons (Part 2) and the bottom of the fuselage (Part 1) so that the helicopter will sit level after completion. Use carpenter's glue and 1¾″ (19 mm) finishing nails to secure these parts together. Counterset the nails, fill the nail holes and sand smooth to prepare for finishing.

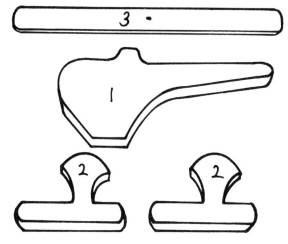

Illus. 5.6   Lay out and cut the helicopter parts.

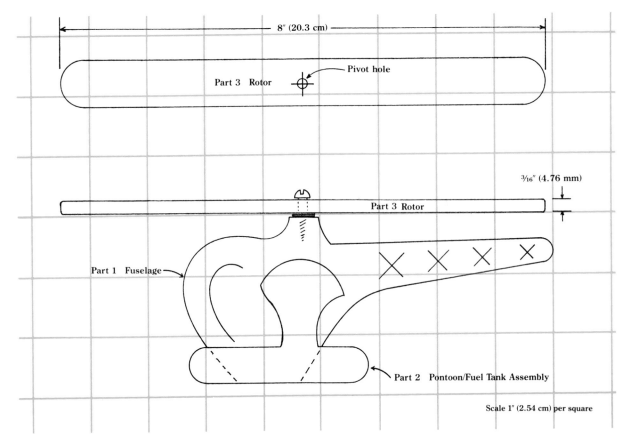

Illus. 5.7   Rescue Helicopter diagram.

3. To make the helicopter rotor (Part 3), rip a piece of material to a thickness of ³⁄₁₆″ (4.76 mm) and lay out the shape of the rotor on this material. Cut it to shape and drill the pivot hole in the center. Sand to a smooth finish.

4. Drill a screw pilot-hole into the center of the rotor mounting-platform at the top of the helicopter.

5. The helicopter should be painted at this time, before the rotor installation. Use non-toxic paints with your choice of colors. This toy also looks very nice if the markings are burned into the wood with a wood-burning set, and then clear varnish is used for the finish.

6. After the painting is finished, the rotor can be installed with a No. 6 × 1″ (2.54 cm) roundhead woodscrew. Place a small flat washer between the helicopter's fuselage and the rotor to act as a bearing surface, and to improve the free spinning of the rotor.

The Rescue Helicopter is now finished. It's time to turn her over to her new pilot and send them out to patrol the coast. I'm sure they'll have hours of fun together.

Navy Sea Plane

Materials List

¾″ (19 mm) hardwood stock,   4″ × 20″
                             (10.16 cm ×
                             50 cm)
Carpenter's glue . . . . small container
1¾″ (4.45 cm) finishing nails, small box
No. 6 × 1″ (2.54 cm)
   roundhead woodscrews . . . 2
No. 6 flat washers 2
¾″ (19 mm) wire brads . . . . . 1 small box
Nontoxic paint: colors of your choice in small
containers

Illus. 5.8

Cutting List

Part 1 . . . Fuselage . . . . Make 1
Part 2 . . . Wing . . . . Make 1
Part 3 . . . Tail . . . . Make 1
Part 4 . . . Engine . . . . Make 2
Part 5 . . . Pontoon . . . . Make 2
Part 6 . . . Propeller . . . . Make 2

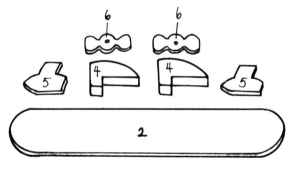

Instructions

LAYOUT

1. Lay out the fuselage (Part 1) and two engines (Part 4) on ¾″ (19 mm) material (Illus. 5.9). Cut these three parts to shape and sand to a smooth finish.
2. The remainder of the ¾″ (19 mm) stock must be ripped down to thinner stock as indicated on Illus. 5.10 and 5.11 for layout of the remaining parts.
3. Lay out the wing (Part 2), the tail (Part 3) and the two pontoons (Part 5) on ⅜″ (9.52

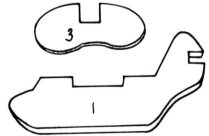

Illus. 5.9   Navy Sea Plane parts.

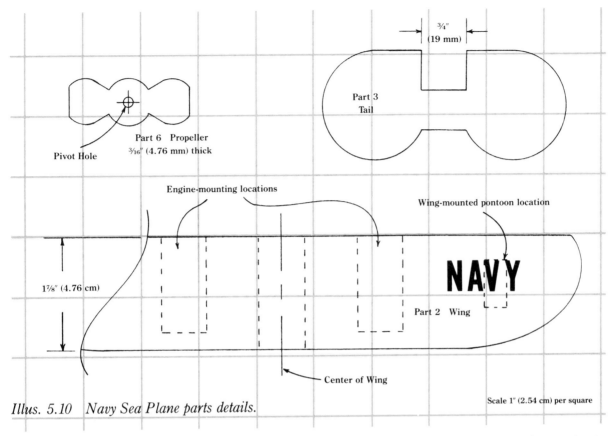

Illus. 5.10   Navy Sea Plane parts details.

mm) material (Illus. 5.9). Cut these parts out with a bandsaw or jigsaw and sand them smooth.

4. Lay out two propellers (Part 6) on material that has been ripped to ³⁄₁₆″ (4.76 mm) thickness (Illus. 5.10).

5. Cut these propellers to shape and sand smooth.

6. Drill the pivot holes into the center of each propeller.

ASSEMBLY

7. Using carpenter's glue and 1¾″ (4.45 cm) finishing nails, assemble the fuselage, wing and tail (Parts 1, 2, and 3) as indicated in Illus. 5.8, 5.10 and 5.11.
   NOTE: Use the location marks shown on the wing (Part 2) in Illus. 5.10 to properly locate the wing (Part 2) to the fuselage (Part 1) and the engines (Part 4) and pontoons (Part 5) to the wing (Part 2).

8. Use carpenter's glue and ¾″ (19 mm) wire brads to mount the engines (Part 4) and the pontoons (Part 5) to the wing (Part 2) as shown in Illus. 5.8 and 5.10.

9. Painting should be done at this time using nontoxic paints of your color choice.

10. To mount the propellers, first drill a small pilot hole into the center of the front side of each engine.

11. Then mount the propellers using No. 6 × 1″ (2.54 cm) roundhead woodscrews. Use a small flat washer as shown in Illus. 5.11 to serve as a bearing surface between the propellers and the engines.
    NOTE: Do not over-tighten the screws so that the propellers cannot spin freely.

The Navy Seaplane is now ready to begin operations in the skies above the seven seas. It could very definitely be used as reconnaissance support for the Naval Air Strike Fleet.

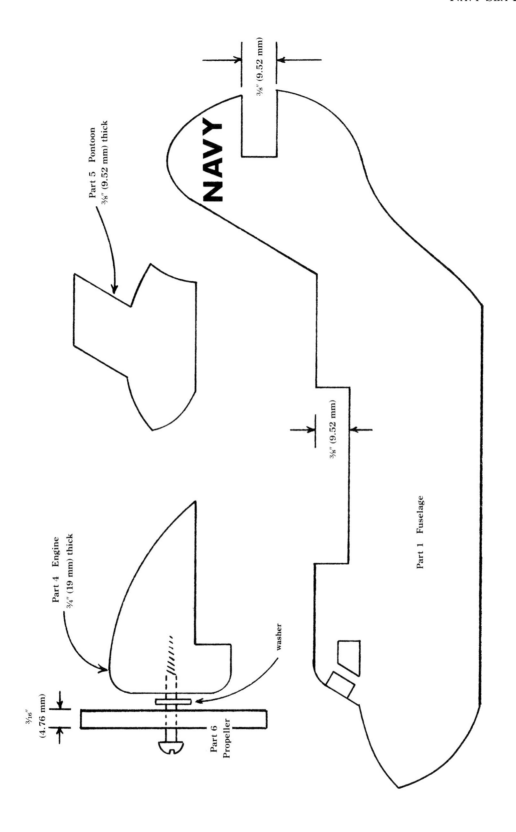

⅜" (9.52 mm)

Part 5   Pontoon
⅜" (9.52 mm) thick

NAVY

⅜" (9.52 mm)

Part 4   Engine
¾" (19 mm) thick

⅜"
(4.76 mm)

washer

Part 6
Propeller

Part 1   Fuselage

Illus. 5.11   Navy Sea Plane diagram. Parts are actual size.

Chapter 6
Early Flying Machines

Twin scenes are being enacted on two different fields. The men involved speak different languages and wear different uniforms. The planes, too, look somewhat different. They have different colors and different markings painted on the wings. The story, however, is much the same: the grassy meadow, a busy crew, the shouts of "Contact!" and then the tiny speck which disappears into the morning sky.

Finally, then, these little war birds meet in a battlefield known only to them. A battlefield high above the earth among the clouds. There they engage in combat: swooping, diving, climbing, turning and spinning, each trying desperately to get the jump on the other, each trying to gain an advantage.

Then suddenly, one engine begins to smoke—oil splashes the pilot's goggles. The plane loses power and its ability to maneuver and is forced down. The victor circles, observing the injured bird as it settles to the ground. He watches the pilot escape to safety. He then passes low overhead in a victory fly-by and offers a salute to his fallen foe, knowing full well that it could as easily have been him.

These infamous rivals of the sky have been recreated here to bring the excitement of this era to life again. They have each been designed with much attention to detail. Sturdy yet simple construction techniques have been implemented to insure many hours of flying fun. The builder, too, is sure to enjoy himself as these classic toys take form.

Triplane

Materials List

*1½" (3.81 cm)-thick hardwood
stock* .... *4½" × 14"
(11.43 cm ×
35.5 cm)*

*⅜" (9.52 mm)-thick hardwood
stock* .... *1½ board feet
(4.57 meters)*

Dowel stock:
½" (12.7 mm) .... *6" (15.24 cm)
length*
⅜" (9.52 mm) .... *9" (22.86 cm)
length*

Illus. 6.1

¼" (6.35 mm) . . . . 15" (38.1 cm)
length

¾" × 2" (19 mm × 5.08
cm) wooden pilot figure . . . 1

1¼" to 1¾" (3.81 to 4.45 cm)
diameter wooden toy wheels, 2

1¾" (4.45 cm) finishing nails, small box

¾" (1.9 cm) wire brads . . . . . small box

No. 8 × 1¼" (3.18 cm)
roundhead woodscrew 1

No. 8 flat washer 1

Carpenter's glue . . . . small container

Nontoxic paint: red, black, brown and white in
small containers

Cutting List

Part 1 . . . Fuselage . . . . Make 1
Part 2 . . . Top Wing . . . . Make 1
Part 3 . . . Middle Wing . . . . Make 1
Part 4 . . . Bottom Wing . . . . Make 1
Part 5 . . . Horizontal Tail . . . . Make 1
Part 6 . . . Vertical Tail . . . . Make 1
Part 7 . . . Propeller . . . . Make 1
Part 8 . . . Tail Skid . . . . Make 1

Instructions

LAYOUT

1. Lay out and cut to shape the fuselage, wings, tail parts, propeller, and tail landing-skid from stock of thickness indicated (Parts 1 through 8, Illus. 6.2, 6.3 and 6.4).

2. Drill a 9⁄32" (7.14 mm) hole in the fuselage (Part 1) for the landing-gear axle to fit through later.

3. Drill two 9⁄32" (7.14 mm) holes up through the landing gear from the bottom of the fuselage (Part 1) as shown in Illus. 6.2. Center these holes at ½" (12.7 mm) apart.

4. Glue two ¼" (6.35 mm) dowels fully into these holes. Cut these dowels and sand the

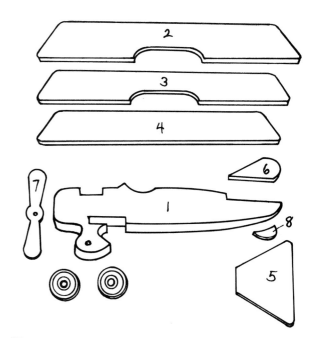

Illus. 6.2 Lay out and cut all the parts for the Triplane.

exposed end smooth. The purpose of these two dowels is to strengthen the landing gear.

WINGS AND TAIL

5. Top wing (Part 2): Drill a 25⁄64" (9.92 mm) hole in each end and four 9⁄32" (7.24 mm) holes near the center of the top wing (Illus. 6.3). Drill these holes from the bottom side of the wing and only halfway through to 3⁄16" (4.76 mm) deep.

6. Center wing (Part 3): Drill all holes as was done in the top wing, except this time drill completely through the wing (Illus. 6.3).

7. Bottom wing (Part 4): Drill 25⁄64" (9.92 mm) holes completely through each end of the bottom wing (Illus. 6.3).

8. Sand all of the above mentioned parts to a smooth pre-finish surface.

9. Place the vertical tail piece (Part 6) into a vise upside down.

10. Center the horizontal tail piece (Part 5) over the vertical tail piece and secure into place with glue and ¾" (19 mm) wire brads (Illus. 6.2 and 6.5).

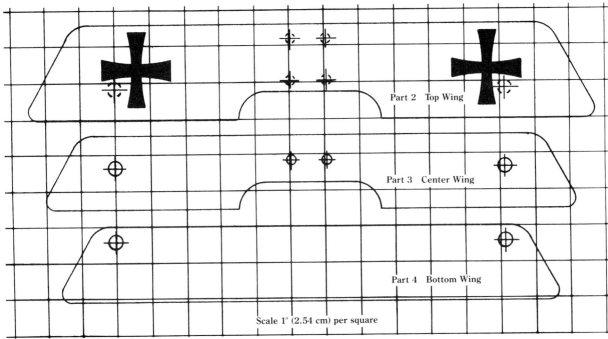

Illus. 6.3   Wings.

11. Place the assembled tail into position on the rear of the fuselage (Part 1) and secure with glue and wire brads. Set brads, fill holes and sand smooth.

12. Secure the bottom wing (Part 4) and the center wing (Part 3) into position with glue and finishing nails, Illus. 6.5. Set nails, fill holes and sand smooth. CAUTION: Be sure the holes at each end of these wings are aligned directly over one another and the two wings are parallel.

13. Cut four sections of ¼″ (6.35 mm) dowel to a length of 1¾″ (4.45 cm) and two sections of ⅜″ (9.52 mm) dowel to a length of 3½″ (8.89 cm). These dowel sections will be wing struts. Sand each end.

14. Place the top wing on the workbench upside down. Glue the four ¼″ (6.35 mm) dowels into the four holes near the center of this wing. Align into a vertical position and allow glue to dry.

15. Glue the two ⅜″ (9.52 mm) wing struts into the holes near the ends of the already installed bottom and center wings (Illus. 6.1). Position these dowels so that they extend through the bottom wing and are flush with the bottom side of this wing.

Illus. 6.4   Install the bottom and center wings. Glue the guns into position.

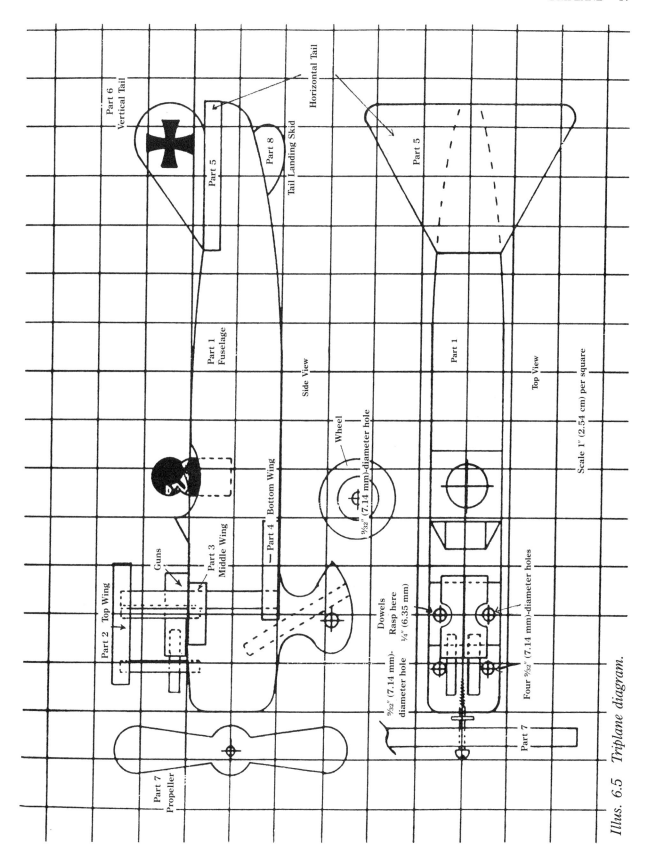

Part 6 Vertical Tail

Part 5

Part 8

Tail Landing Skid

Horizontal Tail

Part 5

Part 1 Fuselage

Part 1

Side View

Top View

Scale 1" (2.54 cm) per square

Guns

Part 3 Middle Wing

Part 2 Top Wing

Part 4 Bottom Wing

Wheel

$^9/_{32}$" (7.14 mm)-diameter hole

Dowels

Rasp here $^1/_4$" (6.35 mm)

$^9/_{32}$" (7.14 mm)-diameter hole

Four $^9/_{32}$" (7.14 mm)-diameter holes

Part 7

Part 7 Propeller

Illus. 6.5   Triplane diagram.

GUNS

16. Cut two ½″ (12.7 mm) dowel sections to a length of 1¾″ (4.45 cm). These will be the gun bodies. Sand each end smooth.
17. Drill a ⁹⁄₃₂″ (7.14 mm) hole into the center of one end of each of these dowels. Drill these holes to a depth of ½″ (12.7 mm).
18. Cut two ¼″ (6.35 mm) dowel sections to 1¼″ (3.18 cm) lengths. Sand each end.
19. Glue the two ¼″ (6.35 mm) dowels fully into the holes in the ½″ (12.7 mm) dowels.
20. Use a round wood rasp to make cuts as indicated in Illus. 6.4 and 6.5 into the ½″ (12.7 mm) dowels so that when they are mounted they will not obstruct the wing strut holes in the top of the fuselage.
21. Glue the two gun assemblies into position (Illus. 6.4).
22. Glue the top wing into position over the guns and check that it is parallel with the other wings (Illus. 6.1).

LANDING GEAR

23. Cut a ¼″ (6.35 mm) dowel section to a length of 2½″ (6.35 cm). This will be the landing-gear axle.
24. Insert the axle through the landing gear hole in the fuselage.
25. Install wooden toy wheels with a drop of glue to each end of the axle. CAUTION: Do not allow glue to get into the axle hole and cause binding.
  NOTE: You may want to complete the painting step before actually gluing the wheels in place.
26. Install the tail landing-skid (Part 8) with glue and wire brads.

PILOT

27. Drill a ¾″ (19 mm) hole to a depth of 1″ (2.54 cm) into the center of the cockpit area.
28. Glue the wooden pilot figure into the cockpit hole. The pilot can be made or purchased through toy parts-supply houses.
  NOTE: You will probably find it easier to paint the pilot before gluing it in place.

PAINTING

29. The most appropriate color for this airplane is bright red.
30. Paint the Iron Cross markings, wheels, propeller and guns black.
31. The markings may be highlighted with white outlines for added character as shown in Illus. 6.1.

PROPELLER

32. Mount the propeller with a roundhead wood screw. Place a small flat washer between the propeller and the fuselage to act as a bearing surface for smoother operation.
33. Do not over-tighten the propeller mounting screw so it won't restrict the propeller spin.

The Triplane is now complete and ready for flight.

Biplane

Materials List

1½" (3.81 cm)-thick hardwood
    stock . . . . 2½" × 12"
                                              (6.35 cm ×
                                              30.5 cm)

⅜" (9.52 mm)-thick hardwood
    stock or ⅜" (9.52 cm)
    veneer plywood . . . . 1½ board feet
                                              (4.57 meters)

Dowel stock
    ½" (12.7 mm) . . . . 6" (15.24 cm)
                                              length
    ⅜" (9.52 mm) . . . . 9" (22.86 cm)
                                              length
    ¼" (6.35 mm) . . . . 15" (38.1 cm)
                                              length

¾" × 2" (19 mm × 5.08
    cm) wooden pilot figure . . . 1

1½" to 1¾" (3.81 cm to 4.45
    cm)-diameter wooden toy
    wheels 2

1¾" (4.45 cm) finishing nails, small box
¾" (19 mm) wire brads . . . . . small box

Illus. 6.6

No. 8 × 1¼" (3.18 cm)
    roundhead woodscrew 1
No. 8 flat washer 8
Carpenter's glue . . . . small container
Nontoxic paint: olive green, tan, black, red,
white, and blue in small containers

Cutting List

Part 1 . . . Fuselage . . . . Make 1
Part 2 . . . Top Wing . . . . Make 1
Part 3 . . . Bottom Wing . . . . Make 1
Part 4 . . . Horizontal Tail . . . . Make 1
Part 5 . . . Vertical Tail . . . . Make 1
Part 6 . . . Landing Gear Strut . . . . Make 2
Part 7 . . . Propeller . . . . Make 1
Part 8 . . . Engine . . . . Make 1
Part 9 . . . Tail Skid . . . . Make 1

Instructions

LAYOUT

1. Lay out and cut the fuselage, wings, tail
   parts, landing gear and tail parts (Parts 1
   through 8) from stock of the thickness indicated in Illus. 6.7, 6.8 and 6.9.

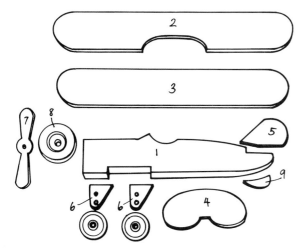

Illus. 6.7   Lay out and cut all parts for the
Biplane.

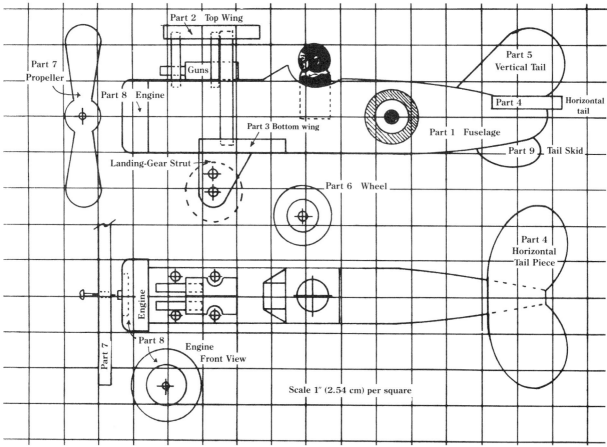

Illus. 6.8   Biplane Diagram.

Illus. 6.9   Wings.

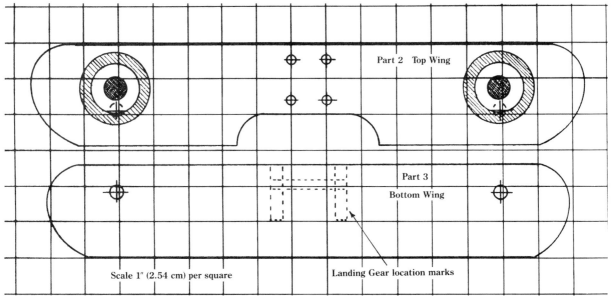

2. Top wing (Part 2): Drill a $^{25}/_{64}''$ (9.92 mm) hole in each end and four $^{9}/_{32}''$ (7.14 mm) holes near the center of the top wing (Illus. 6.9). Drill these holes from the bottom side of the wing and only halfway through, $^{3}/_{16}''$ (4.76 mm) deep.

3. Bottom wing (Part 3): Drill a $^{25}/_{64}''$ (9.92 mm) hole completely through each end of the bottom wing as shown in Illus. 6.9.

4. Sand all of the above-mentioned parts to a smooth pre-finish surface.

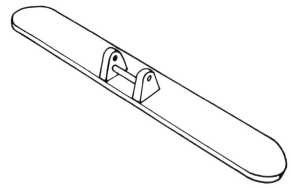

Illus. 6.10   Fabrication of landing gear on bottom wing (upside down view).

ASSEMBLY

5. Use the landing-gear location marks on the bottom wing (Illus. 6.9) to align the two landing-gear struts (Part 6) properly in place.

6. Secure these parts with carpenter's glue and $^{3}/_{4}''$ (19 mm) wire brads.

7. Cut a $^{1}/_{4}''$ (6.35 mm) dowel section $2^{1}/_{4}''$ (5.72 cm) long.

8. Fit this dowel section into the upper hole of each landing-gear strut so that it spans between the two, and glue in place to make a landing-gear brace (Illus. 6.10).

9. Place the vertical tail piece (Part 5) into a vice upside down.

10. Align and center the horizontal tail piece (Part 4) over the vertical tail piece, and secure into position with glue and $^{3}/_{4}''$ (19 mm) wire brads.
    NOTE: The vertical tail piece extends approximately 1″ (2.54 cm) beyond the forward side of the horizontal tail piece or until the back edges are evenly aligned (Illus. 6.8 and 6.11).

11. Place the assembled tail into position on the rear of the fuselage and secure with glue and wire brads. Set the brads, fill the holes and sand smooth.

12. Secure the bottom wing (Part 3) into position with glue and finishing nails. Set nails, fill holes and sand smooth.

WING STRUTS

13. Cut four sections of $^{1}/_{4}''$ (6.35 mm) dowel to a length of $1^{1}/_{4}''$ (3.81 cm) and two sections of $^{3}/_{8}''$ (9.52 mm) dowel to a length of $3^{3}/_{8}''$ (8.57 cm). Sand both ends of each dowel section. These dowels will be used as wing struts.

14. Place the top wing (Part 2) upside down on the workbench. Glue the four $^{1}/_{4}''$ (6.35 mm) dowel sections into the four holes near the center of this wing. Glue the two $^{3}/_{8}''$ (5.2 mm) dowels into the two holes near the end of the wing. Align all of these dowels in a vertical position and allow the glue to set.

GUNS

15. Cut two $^{1}/_{2}''$ (12.7 mm) dowel sections $1^{1}/_{4}''$ (3.81 cm) long. Sand both ends.

16. Drill a $^{9}/_{32}''$ (7.14 mm) hole into the center of one end of each of these $^{1}/_{2}''$ (12.7 mm) dowels. Drill this hole to a depth of $^{1}/_{2}''$ (12.7 mm).

17. Cut two $^{1}/_{4}''$ (6.35 mm) dowel sections to a length of $1^{1}/_{4}''$ (3.18 cm). Sand both ends.

18. Glue the two ¼″ (6.35 mm) dowel into the holes in the ½″ (12.7 mm) dowels (Illus. 6.8).

19. Use a round wood rasp to make cuts into each ½″ (12.7 mm) dowel as shown in the top view of Illus. 6.8 so that when these parts are mounted in place, the 9⁄32″ (7.14 mm) holes in the front of the fuselage will not be covered by the gun bodies.

20. Glue the two gun assemblies in place on the fuselage.

21. Glue the top wing in place above the guns, fitting all the wing struts into the respective holes on the fuselage and the bottom wing. Align the top wing so that it is parallel to the bottom wing. Allow the glue to dry (Illus. 6.6).

LANDING GEAR

22. Cut a ¼″ (6.35 mm) dowel section to a length of 3⅜″ (8.57 cm) to serve as the landing gear axle.

23. Insert this dowel through the lower holes in the landing gear struts.

24. Install wooden toy wheels to each end of the axle with a drop of glue. CAUTION: Do not allow the glue to get into the axle hole and cause binding.
    NOTE: You may want to wait until after the painting step to actually install the wheels.

25. Use glue and wire brads to secure the tail skid (Part 9) into place.

ENGINE

26. To form the engine and cowling (Part 8), drill a shallow 1⅛″ (2.86 cm)-diameter hole into a piece of ¾″ (19 mm) stock. Center a 2¼″ (5.72 cm) hole saw over this shallow hole and saw completely through the stock. Use a rasp to round the front edge of the engine cowling (Illus. 6.8). Sand this part to a pre-finish surface.

Illus. 6.11   Installation of tail section and painting details.

27. Position the engine (Part 8) on the front of the fuselage and secure with glue and finishing nails (Illus. 6.6). Set nails, fill holes and sand smooth.

28. Mount the propeller (Part 7) into position with a roundhead wood screw. Use several flat washers to space the propeller away from the engine cowling so that they do not touch. Do not over-tighten the screw and restrict propeller operation.
    NOTE: The propeller should be removed again when painting the plane.

PILOT

29. Drill a ¾″ (19 mm) hole into the center of the cockpit area (Illus. 6.8). Drill to a depth of 1″ (2.54 cm).

30. Glue a wooden pilot figure into this hole.
    NOTE: You will probably want to paint the pilot before actually gluing it into place.

PAINTING

31. The entire plane should be painted olive green and tan, camouflage-fashion.

32. The wheels, engine and guns are to be painted black.

33. The bull's eyes are red, white and blue.

The Biplane is complete and ready for its maiden flight.

Chapter 7
The Space Fleet Shooting Stars

Now we shall move on beyond the sky and the roar of radial engines, for the boundaries of the sky no longer exist for us. It is in the midst of the stars that these spacecraft reign as the celestial peace keepers of the universe.

The Star Defender is powered by two powerful ion thrusters and is armed with a trio of short-range laser cannons. She is perfectly suited for patrolling and protecting the local galaxy and its planets. Her sleek design makes her capable of blistering speeds yet she is highly maneuverable when engaged in dog fights. With computer-controlled guidance and defense systems, she poses a threat to invaders that cannot be ignored.

With its long-range capabilities, the Star Patroller can take over where the Star Defender turns back. Its three laser cannons are equipped with energy intensifiers which allow it to reach further and hit harder than its sister ship. It is propelled through the depths of space by three proton thrusters at speeds that can hardly be imagined, yet maneuverability in close combat is one of its best virtues. The bullet-like design of this magnificent machine has been sharply interrupted by a large nose compartment—a device completely filled with sensitive surveillance equipment that leaves nothing unnoticed as it searches out the would-be invaders. Space station inhabitants can rest more easily knowing this watchdog of the stars is on the job.

Each of these space fighters can be constructed within a few hours. They are fun to build and fun for any young space cadet to own.

Star Defender

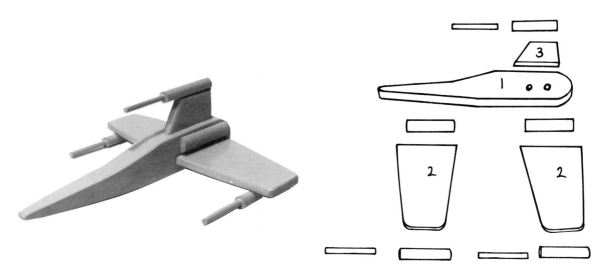

Illus. 7.1

Illus. 7.2   Layout of parts for Star Defender.

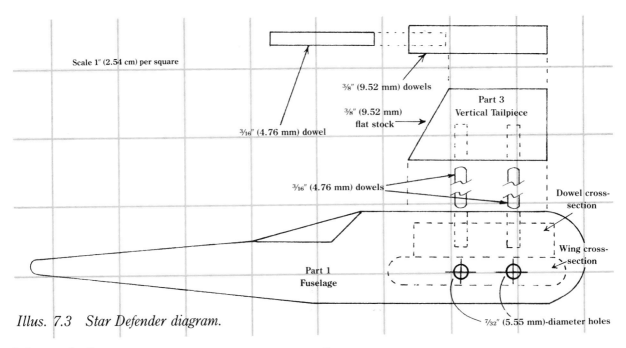

Illus. 7.3   Star Defender diagram.

Materials List

1" (2.54 cm)-thick hardwood
*   stock* .... *1½" × 9"*
*   (3.81 cm ×*
*   22.86 cm)*

⅜" (9.52 mm)-thick hardwood
*   stock* .... *3" × 10" (7.62*
*   cm × 25.4 cm)*

Dowel stock:
*   ⅜" (9.52 mm) diameter* .. *6" (15.24 cm)*
*   length*
*   ³⁄₁₆" (4.76 mm) diameter* .. *14" (35.56 cm)*
*   length*
*   ½" (1.27 cm) diameter* ... *3" (7.62 cm)*
*   length*

Carpenter's glue .... *small container*
¾" (19 mm) wire brads ..... *small box*
Nontoxic paint: your choice of colors in small
containers

Cutting List

Part 1 ... *Fuselage* .... *Make 1*
Part 2 ... *Wing* .... *Make 2*
Part 3 ... *Vertical Tail* .... *Make 1*

Instructions

LAYOUT

1. Lay out and cut to shape the fuselage (Part 1), the vertical tail piece (Part 3) and two wing sections (Part 2) as shown in Illus. 7.3, 7.4 and 7.5.

2. Drill the ⁷⁄₃₂" (5.55 mm) assembly holes into each of these parts as indicated in Illus. 7.3 and 7.4.

3. Sand all of the parts to a smooth pre-finish surface.

4. Cut two sections of ³⁄₁₆" (4.76 mm) doweling to 2⅜" (6.03 cm) length and two sections to ¾" (19 mm) length. Sand both ends of each of the dowel sections.

ASSEMBLY

5. Assemble the wing sections (Part 2) and the vertical tail piece (Part 3) to the fuselage (Part 1) using the dowel sections in Step 4 as guide pins as shown in Illus. 7.3 and 7.4. Secure these assembled parts with glue, align them carefully and allow the glue to dry completely without disturbing the assembly.

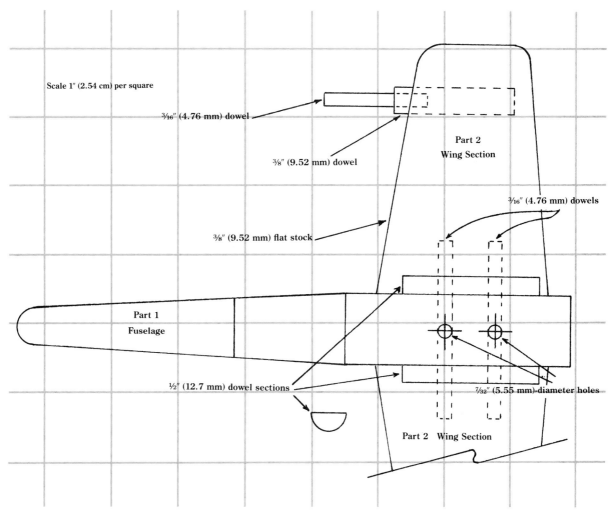

Illus. 7.4   Top view of Star Defender.

6. To assemble the laser cannons, first cut three sections of ³/₈″ (9.52 mm) dowel 2″ (5.08 cm) long. Sand each end.

7. Drill a ⁷/₃₂″ (5.55 mm) hole into the center of one end of each of these ³/₈″ (9.52 mm) dowels to a depth of ½″ (12.7 mm) (Illus. 7.3 and 7.4).

8. Cut three sections of ³/₁₆″ (4.76 mm) doweling 1½″ (3.81 cm) long. Sand each end.

9. Glue the ³/₁₆″ (4.76 mm) dowel sections fully into the holes drilled in Step 7 in the ³/₈″ (9.52 mm) dowels.

10. Install these laser cannon assemblies as indicated in Illus. 7.1, 7.3 and 7.4. Secure in place with glue and ¾″ (19 mm) wire brads.

11. The thrusters are made with a piece of ½″ (12.7 mm) doweling 2″ (5.08 cm) long.

12. Split this dowel section exactly in half as shown in Illus. 7.4 using a band saw or jig saw. Sand the saw-cut surfaces smooth.

13. Glue the thruster to each side of the fuselage just above the wings as shown in Illus. 7.1, 7.3 and 7.4.

14. Nontoxic paints of your color choice can be used to paint the toy at this time.

The Star Defender is finished and can be turned over to its space pilot.

Star Patroller

Materials List

1¼" (3.18 cm)-thick hardwood stock .... *2" × 12" (5.08 cm × 30.48 cm)*

⅜" (9.52 mm)-thick hardwood stock .... *4" × 8" (10.16 cm × 20.32 cm)*

5/16" (7.93 mm)-thick hardwood stock .... *2" × 6" (5.08 cm × 15.24 cm)*

Dowel stock:
   ½" (12.7 mm) diameter .. *15" (38.1 cm) long*
   3/16" (4.76 mm) diameter .. *15" (38.1 cm) long*

Wooden golf tee *3*
Carpenter's glue .... *small container*
1¾" (4.45 cm) finishing nails, small box
¾" (19 mm) wire brads ..... *small box*
Nontoxic paint: your choice of colors in small containers

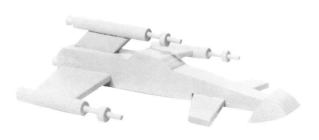

Illus. 7.5

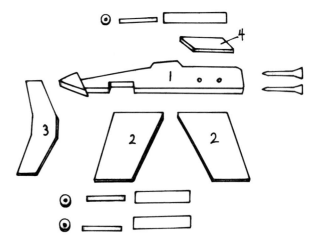

Illus. 7.6   Star Patroller parts.

Cutting List

Part 1 ... Fuselage .... *Make 1*
Part 2 ... Wing .... *Make 2*
Part 3 ... Forward Control Wing, Make 1
Part 4 ... Vertical Tail .... *Make 1*

Instructions

LAYOUT

1. Lay out and cut to shape the fuselage (Part 1), two wing sections (Part 2), the forward control wing (Part 3) and the vertical tail piece (Part 4) from hardwood stock of the thicknesses shown in Illus. 7.7 and 7.8. These parts and the others needed are also depicted in Illus. 7.6.

2. Sand all of these parts to a smooth pre-finish surface.

3. Drill the 7/32" (5.55 mm) assembly holes into Parts 1 and 2 as indicated on the drawings. Also drill the two holes of the same size for

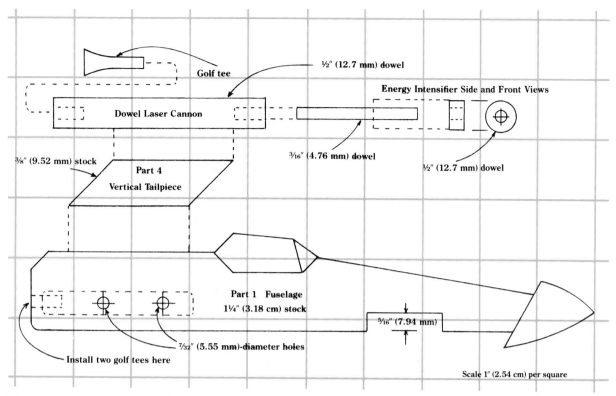

Illus. 7.7 Star Patroller diagram.

the thrusters in the rear of the fuselage. Drill the thruster holes to a depth of ½″ (12.7 mm).

BODY AND WINGS

4. Cut two sections of ³⁄₁₆″ (4.76 mm) dowel to a length of 2½″ (6.35 cm). Sand each end.

5. Assemble the wings (Part 2) to the fuselage (Part 1) using these dowels as guide pins (Illus. 7.8).

6. Glue these parts together, align carefully and set the entire assembly aside until the glue is completely dry.

7. Install the forward control wing (Part 3) to the fuselage (Part 1) with the use of glue and ¾″ (19 mm) wire brads (Illus. 7.8).

8. Install the vertical tail piece (Part 4) to the fuselage (Part 1) by gluing and nailing with 1¾″ (4.45 cm) finishing nails. Pre-drill the nail holes in Part 4 to prevent splitting.

9. The thrusters are made from golf tees with the pointed end cut off. Prepare two such tees at this time and glue them into the holes at the rear of the fuselage. Align carefully and allow the glue to dry.

LASER CANNON

10. The center laser cannon is made from a section of ½″ (12.7 mm) dowel cut to a length of 3½″ (8.89 cm). Sand each end.

11. Drill a ⁷⁄₃₂″ (5.55 mm)-diameter hole into the center of each end of this dowel to a depth of ½″ (12.7 mm).

12. Glue a shortened golf tee into one of the holes, following the directions for the other two thrusters in Step 9.

13. The two wing-tip laser cannons are also made with ½″ (12.7 mm) dowel, but they are to be cut at only 3″ (7.62 cm) lengths.

14. These two dowels will have a ⁷⁄₃₂″ (5.55

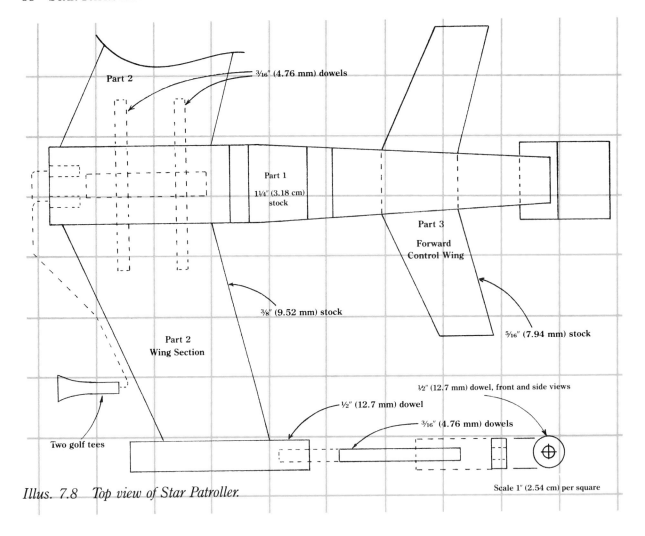

Illus. 7.8   Top view of Star Patroller.

mm) hole drilled into the center of one end only. These holes, too, are to be drilled ½" (12.7 mm) deep.

15. Now, cut three 2" (5.08 cm) sections of ³⁄₁₆" (4.76 mm) dowel. Sand each end.

16. Glue these dowel sections fully into the holes at the ends of the laser cannons. Allow the glue to dry completely.

17. To make the laser cannon energy intensifiers, start with a section of ½" (12.7 mm) dowel, several inches long.

18. Drill a ⁷⁄₃₂" (5.55 mm)-diameter hole in the center of one end of this dowel to a depth of an inch or so.

19. Now cut three wafers from the end of this dowel that has the hole drilled into it. These wafers should be ¼" (6.35 mm) in thickness. CAUTION: Use a jigsaw or a small handsaw for this operation for safety's sake.

20. Sand these parts well and glue them in place on the ³⁄₁₆" (4.76 mm) dowel cannon barrels as shown in Illus. 7.5, 7.7 and 7.8.

21. Install the three complete laser cannon assemblies in place with the use of ¾" (19 mm) wire brads and carpenter's glue.

22. The project can now be painted with non-toxic paints of your choosing.

The Star Patroller can now join the Star Defender to protect our planet.

Chapter 8
On Safari

As grey dawn replaced the darkness of night across the North African plains, a lion crouched in the golden-colored grass watching a herd of Kudu antelope feeding before him. Soon one of the Kudus drifted away from the herd toward where the lion hid. The lion calculated the distance and sprang from the cover of the tall grass. Startled by the sudden movement, the young antelope broke into a hard run with the lion close behind.

Then, just at the moment when the lion was ready to leap for the Kudu's throat, they broke from behind some brush directly across the path of a large bull elephant. This time it was the lion who was startled and whose concentration was broken by the sheer size and sudden appearance of the elephant, allowing the Kudu to escape.

The projects in this chapter will allow your youngsters to recreate this wildlife adventure on the North African plains for themselves, or to enact others in the three-ringed circus. These profile toys have been designed as simple take-apart puzzles to add to their enjoyment.

African Lion

Materials List

¾" (19 mm)-thick hardwood
 stock . . . . 1 board foot (3
 meters)
⅜" (9.52 mm)-diameter
 hardwood dowel . . . . 6" (15.24 cm)
Carpenter's glue . . . . small container
Dark wood stain . . . . small container
Clear varnish . . . . small container

Cutting List

Part 1 . . . Body . . . . Make 1
Part 2 . . . Foreleg . . . . Make 2
Part 3 . . . Hindleg . . . . Make 2
Part 4 . . . Mane . . . . Make 1

Illus. 8.1

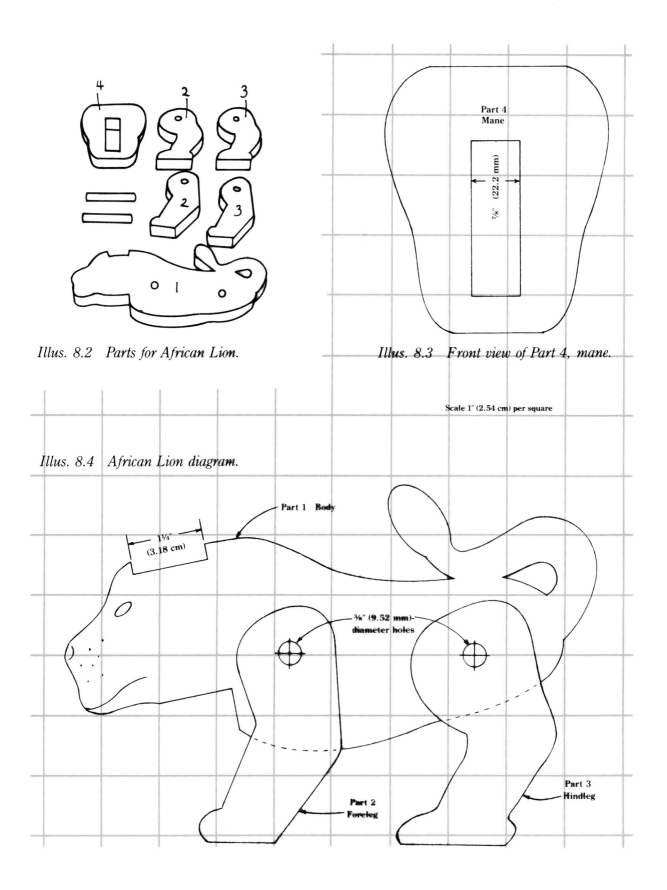

Illus. 8.2   Parts for African Lion.

Illus. 8.3   Front view of Part 4, mane.

Part 4
Mane

7/8" (22.2 mm)

Scale 1" (2.54 cm) per square

Illus. 8.4   African Lion diagram.

Part 1   Body

1¼" (3.18 cm)

3/8" (9.52 mm)-diameter holes

Part 2   Foreleg

Part 3   Hindleg

Instructions

LAYOUT

1. Lay out and cut to shape the body (Part 1), two forelegs (Part 2), two hind legs (Part 3) and the mane (Part 4) using ¾″ (19 mm) hardwood stock (Illus. 8.2, 8.3 and 8.4).

2. Drill ⅜″ (9.52 mm)-diameter holes into the body (Part 1) and into all the legs (Parts 2 and 3) at the points indicated in Illus. 8.4.

3. Cut two sections of ⅜″ (9.52 mm)-diameter dowel to 2½″ (6.35 cm) in length.

4. Sand all of the above-mentioned parts to a smooth pre-finish surface.

5. Using carpenter's glue, glue the two dowel sections into the holes in the body (Part 1) so that they are centered and extend through each side of the body in an equal amount. Allow the glue to dry completely.

6. Using a dark wood-stain such as walnut, dark oak or the like, stain the mane (Part 4) and the tip of the tail on Part 1 to a dark shade.

7. Mark the facial features into Part 1 with a wood-burning set.

8. Varnish all of the parts with a nontoxic clear varnish. Allow to dry.

9. Assemble the lion by simply pressing the legs (Parts 2 and 3) into place on the extended dowels, and by placing the mane over the head and fitting it into the notch provided for it. Do not use glue on these parts. They are designed to be removable as a puzzle.

The African Lion is now completed. You can go on to build his companion, the Bull Elephant.

Bull Elephant

Materials List

¾″ (19 mm)-thick hardwood
  stock . . . . *1½ board feet (4.57 meters)*

Hardwood dowel:
  ⅜″ (9.52 mm) diameter . . *6″ (15.24 cm)*
  ¼″ (6.35 mm) diameter . . *6″ (15.24 cm)*
Carpenter's glue . . . . *small container*
Nontoxic paint (light grey) . . . *small container*

Cutting List

Part 1	*. . . Body . . . .*	*Make 1*
Part 2	*. . . Foreleg . . . .*	*Make 2*
Part 3	*. . . Hind leg . . . .*	*Make 2*
Part 4	*. . . Ear . . . .*	*Make 2*
Part 5	*. . . Tusk . . . .*	*Make 2*

Illus. 8.5

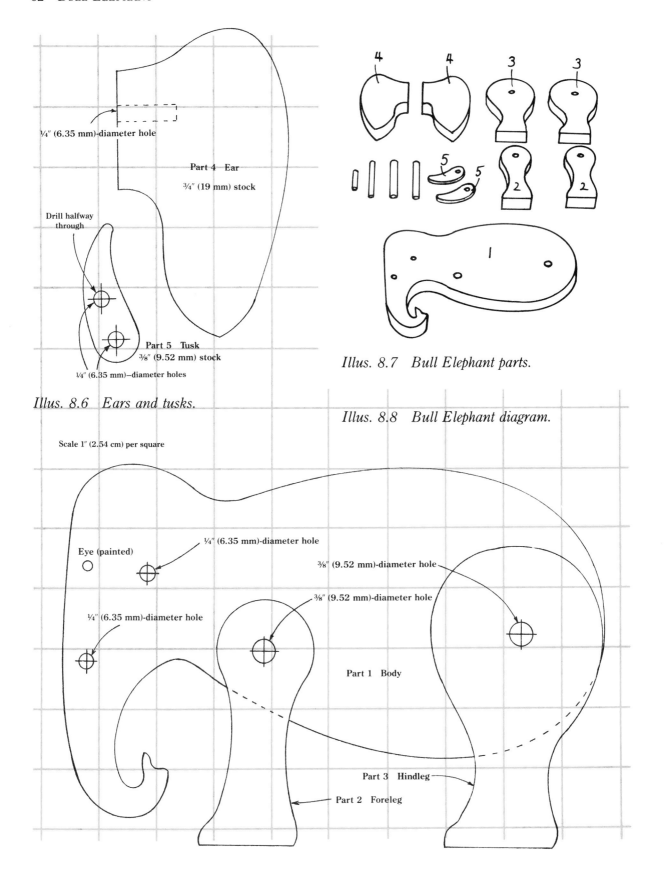

¼″ (6.35 mm)-diameter hole

Part 4 Ear

¾″ (19 mm) stock

Drill halfway
through

Part 5 Tusk

⅜″ (9.52 mm) stock

¼″ (6.35 mm)–diameter holes

Illus. 8.6 Ears and tusks.

Illus. 8.7 Bull Elephant parts.

Illus. 8.8 Bull Elephant diagram.

Scale 1″ (2.54 cm) per square

Eye (painted)

¼″ (6.35 mm)-diameter hole

⅜″ (9.52 mm)-diameter hole

⅜″ (9.52 mm)-diameter hole

¼″ (6.35 mm)-diameter hole

Part 1 Body

Part 3 Hindleg

Part 2 Foreleg

Instructions

LAYOUT

1. Lay out and cut to shape the body (Part 1), two forelegs (Part 2), two hind legs (Part 3) and two ears (Part 4) on ¾″ (19 mm) hardwood stock (Illus. 8.6, 8.7 and 8.8).

2. Lay out and cut to shape the two tusks (Part 5) from ⅜″ (9.52 mm) material (Illus. 8.6). This material can be made by ripping a small piece of ¾″ (19 mm) material.

3. Drill the ⅜″ (9.52 mm) holes at the appropriate locations on Parts 1, 2 and 3 for the leg-mounting dowels to fit into (Illus. 8.8).

4. Drill ¼″ (6.35 mm) holes in Parts 1, 4, and 5 as shown in the drawings.
   NOTE: The hole in Part 4 should be drilled to a depth of 1″ (2.54 cm) and the hole nearest the pointed end of Part 5 should only be drilled halfway through the part or ³⁄₁₆″ (4.76 mm) from the inside.

5. Cut two ⅜″ (9.52 mm)-diameter dowels and one ¼″ (6.35 mm)-diameter dowel to a length of 2½″ (6.35 cm).

6. Cut one ¼″ (6.35 mm) dowel section to a length of 1½″ (3.81 cm).

7. Cut two sections of ¼″ (6.35 mm) dowel to a length of ⅜″ (9.52 mm).

8. Sand all parts to a smooth pre-finish surface.

ASSEMBLY

9. Use carpenter's glue for the assembly steps.

10. Glue the shortest ¼″ (6.35 mm) dowel sections into the holes nearest the pointed end of each tusk (Illus. 8.6).

11. Glue the remaining dowel sections into the leg holes in the body so that they are centered and extend an equal amount on each side.
    NOTE: The shortest remaining dowel section, the one from Step 6, should be assembled into the tusk mounting-hole.

12. Paint all parts with a light grey, nontoxic paint, except the tusks, which should be painted white.

13. Paint the eyes with black paint.

14. Assemble by pressing each piece onto the appropriate dowels: do not use glue (Illus. 8.5).

This completes the Bull Elephant and adds still another nice toy to your collection or that of some youngster in your life.

Chapter 9
Naval Air-Strike Fleet

"Captain, C.I.C. reports two bogies approaching. . . . bearing . . . 2 . . . 7 . . . 3, speed . . . 600 knots, range . . . 850 miles."

"Sound general quarters; alert the fleet; prepare to launch two interceptors."

The well-trained crews of five ships move quickly and efficiently to their battle stations. In under two minutes all five ships are ready to do battle, should it be necessary. Guns are ready to fire; missiles are ready to launch and the pilots of two F-14 Tomcat jet fighters are buckled into place . . . jet engines running . . . catapult gear hooked up . . . waiting for the order to fly.

The five ships are on routine training maneuvers in the South Pacific. The flag ship is a modern aircraft carrier outfitted with several squadrons of fighter and attack aircraft. She has a crew of more than 5000 men and is a floating military air base.

The fleet also includes a giant battleship equipped with nine 20″ (50 cm) guns that can fire rounds accurately for more than 20 miles or 32 kilometers. This floating fortress has an array of smaller artillery for doing battle at closer quarters.

A landing ship is here for the purpose of delivering the infantry forces to shore along with their trucks, tanks and other heavy equipment. It can run right up to the beach and open its large bow gate so that the equipment can be driven on to the beach accompanied by a battalion of foot soldiers. It also has a heliport on the stern so that other supplies can be flown ashore.

They are protected from attack by sea by a patrolling submarine. This underwater vessel can fire torpedos at enemy surface ships or fire missiles at their land bases. Its invisibility makes it a real threat.

The last ship of this fleet is also the smallest, but a real work horse. The destroyer can fire nine-inch guns in ship-to-ship surface battles. It is outfitted with anti-aircraft batteries for air defense and can go after intruder submarines with sonar equipment and depth charges.

These five ships have been recreated here and designed for construction in your home workshop. Realistic detail has been made an integral part of each one. I'm sure you will find real pleasure in bringing these Navy vessels into existence for some young Fleet Admiral.

Play House Range.
See pp. 90–93.

Play House Kitchen Sink.
See pp. 94–97.

Little Chair. See pp. 100–101.

Little House. See pp. 7–14.

Rocking Horse. See pp. 15–19.

A

Triplane. See pp. 44–48.

Bush Plane. See pp. 36–38.

Rescue Helicopter. See pp. 39–40.

Grand Prix Racer.
See pp. 29–31.

B

Road Grader. See pp. 124–127.

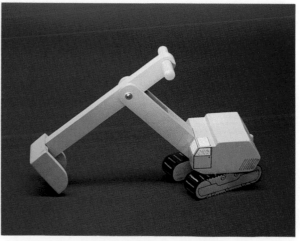

Construction Digger. See pp. 115–118.

Backhoe. See pp. 109–114.

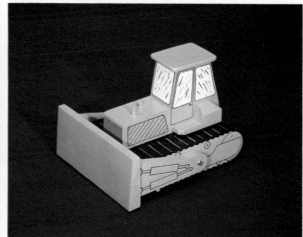

Bulldozer. See pp. 104–108.

*Two views of Dump Truck.
See pp. 119–123.*

C

Star Patroller (left) and Star Defender. See pp. 56–58 and pp. 53–55.

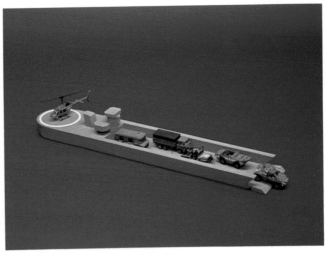

Landing Ship. See pp. 78–81.

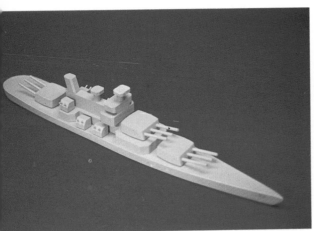

Battleship. See pp. 69–74.

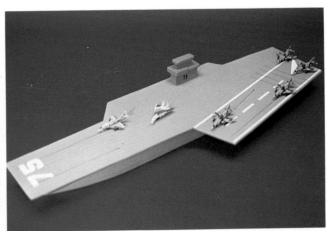

Aircraft Carrier. See pp. 65–68.

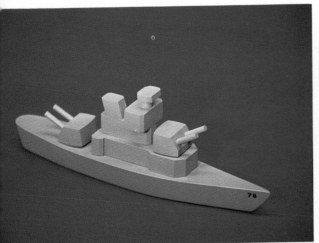

Naval Destroyer. See pp. 82–85.

Submarine. See pp. 75–77.

Aircraft Carrier

Materials List

Lumber . . . . *2½″ × 6″ × 36″ (6.35 cm × 15.24 cm × 91.44 cm)*

¼″ (6.35 mm)-thick veneer
  plywood . . . . *15″ × 36″ (38.1 cm × 91.44 cm)*

¾″ (19 mm) hardwood stock, *½ board foot (1.5 meters)*

Carpenter's glue . . . . *small container*

¾″ (19 mm) wire brads . . . . . *small box*

No. 6 × ¾″ (19 mm)
  flathead woodscrews *2*

Nontoxic paint:
  Battleship grey . . . . *1 pint*
  White . . . . *small amount*
  Black . . . . *small amount*
Metal airplane miniatures . . . *1 or 2 sets*

Cutting List

Part 1 . . . Hull . . . . Make 1
Part 2 . . . Flight Deck . . . . Make 1
Part 3 . . . Island Part A . . . . Make 1
Part 4 . . . Island Part B . . . . Make 1
Part 5 . . . Island Part C . . . . Make 1
Part 6 . . . Island Part D . . . . Make 1
Part 7 . . . Island Part E . . . . Make 1

Instructions

HULL

1. The hull should be cut from the 2½″ × 6″ × 36″ (6.35 cm × 15.24 cm × 91.44 cm) piece of wood (Illus. 9.2). The thickness of this part may be built up by laminating sev-

Illus. 9.1

eral pieces of thinner wood together. The 2½″ (6.35 cm) dimension is not extremely critical. It may vary by ¼″ (6.35 mm) to ⅜″ (9.52 mm) in either direction.

2. Lay out the hull shape onto the top of this laminated section of wood.

3. Set bandsaw- or jigsaw-table to an angle of 10°.

4. Cut the entire perimeter of the hull so that the upper face will be the larger side. This will give the finished shape of the ship's hull (Illus. 9.3).

5. Sand the hull section thoroughly to give a finished appearance. Radius the bottom edges so as to eliminate sharp corners.

6. The finished hull may now be painted battleship grey.

FLIGHT DECK

7. The material for this part is ¼″ (6.35 mm) plywood, 15″ (38.1 cm) wide and 36″ (91.44 cm) long.

8. Lay out the shape of the flight deck onto the plywood (Illus. 9.4).

9. Cut the entire perimeter with a bandsaw or jigsaw. Sand the deck for finishing.

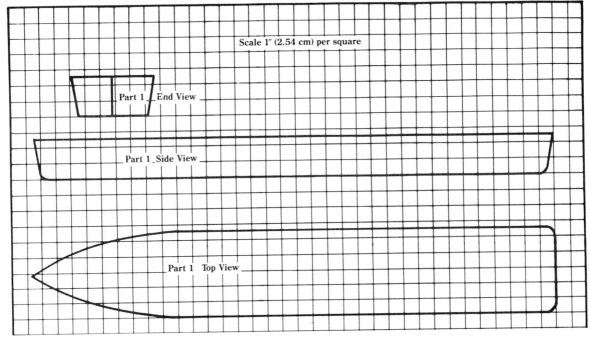

Illus. 9.2   Top, side and end view of Part 1, hull.

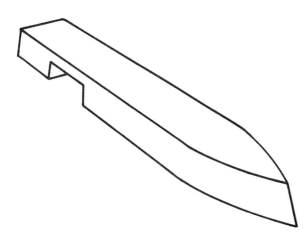

Illus. 9.3   Ship's hull viewed from upside down position.

10. The flight deck should be painted battleship grey at this time.

11. Lay out the markings onto the painted deck (Illus. 9.5). The landing area markings may be masked with tape and painted white.

12. After the white paint is dry, remove masking tape and mask catapult tracks and arresting gear. These marks should be painted black (Illus. 9.4).

13. After the black paint is dry, the flight deck is completely finished. Set aside until ready for assembly.

ISLAND

14. Lay out and cut the various parts of the island (Illus. 9.7).

15. Sand all parts for finishing.

16. Paint the parts battleship grey.

17. After the paint is completely dry, use masking tape to put the ship's number on both sides of the island base and paint white.

18. The island may now be assembled using wood glue and ¾″ (19 mm) wire brads. Countersink brads and fill the holes.

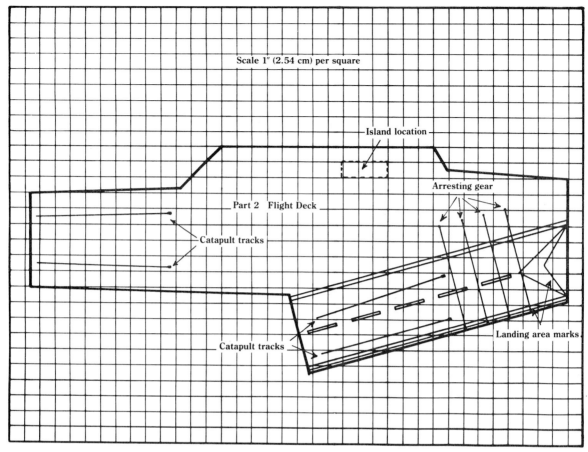

Illus. 9.4   Part 2, flight deck, with painting guide.

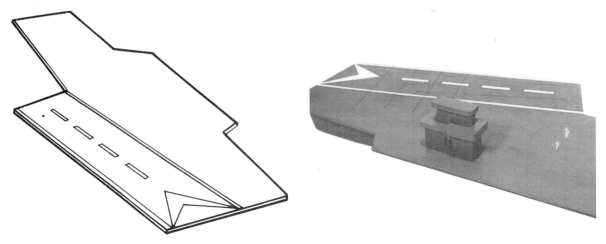

Illus. 9.5   Painted flight deck.

Illus. 9.6   Flight deck mounted on hull.

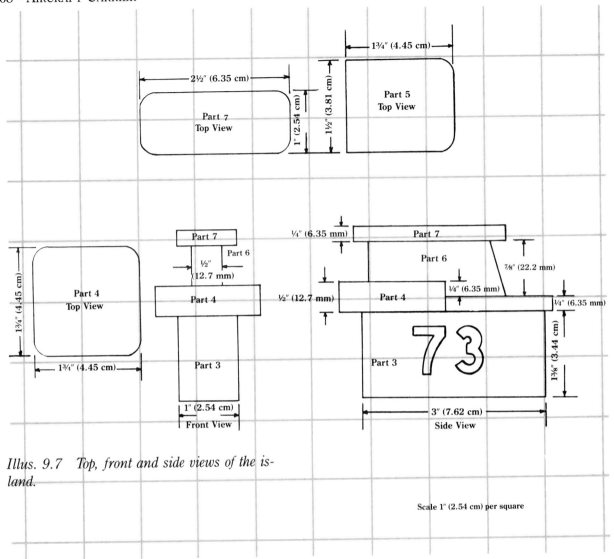

Illus. 9.7 Top, front and side views of the is-land.

Scale 1″ (2.54 cm) per square

ASSEMBLY

19. Locate the flight deck on the hull assembly. Secure in place with glue and wire brads. Countersink and fill the holes (Illus. 9.6).
20. Locate the island on the flight deck. Secure with glue and two small screws form the bottom side of the flight deck (Illus. 9.1).
21. Touch-up all the filled nail holes with paint.

Your Aircraft Carrier is now completed. If you want to give it a name, the name should be painted with small, black letters across the stern (rear) of the ship's hull. A good choice for the name is the child's name for whom it was built, for example "USS David C. Randolf."

To outfit this ship with a squadron of airplanes, purchase a set or two of die-cast metal miniature airplanes.

Battleship

Materials List

1¼" (3.18 cm)-thick
   hardwood stock .... 5" × 31" (12.7
                          cm × 78.74
                          cm)

¾" (19 mm)-thick hardwood
   stock .... 1½ board feet
                          (4.57 meters)

Hardwood dowel:
   ½" (12.7 cm) diameter ... 3" (7.62 cm)
   ¼" (6.35 mm) diameter .. 30" (76.2 cm)
   ⅛" (3.18 mm) diameter .. 15" (38.1 cm)

No. 8 × 1¼" (3.18 cm)
   roundhead woodscrews ... 6

No. 8 × 1" (2.54 cm)
   roundhead woodscrews ... 3

¼" (6.35 mm) fender washers, 3

¼" (6.35 mm) flat washers .. 6

Carpenter's glue .... small container

1½" (3.81 cm) finishing
   nails .... small box

Nontoxic paint:
   Battleship grey .... 1 pint
   White .... small amount

Cutting List

Part 1 ... Hull .... Make 1
Part 2 ... Lower Superstructure .. Make 1
Part 3 ... Upper Superstructure ... Make 1
Part 4 ... Conning Tower .... Make 1
Part 5 ... Bridge .... Make 1
Part 6 ... Forward Radar .... Make 1
Part 7 ... Aft Radar .... Make 1
Part 8 ... Stack .... Make 1
Part 9 ... Large Gun Turret ..... Make 3
Part 10 .. Small Gun Turret ..... Make 6

Illus. 9.8

Instructions

Read instructions completely before starting.

HULL

1. Use the piece of wood 1¼" (3.18 cm) thick, 5" (12.7 cm) wide and 31" (78.74 cm) long.
2. Lay out the outline of the hull (Part 1) onto this piece of wood (Illus. 9.9).
3. Set the bandsaw or jigsaw at an angle of 12°.
4. Cut the entire perimeter of the hull so that the upward face is the largest side. This will give the finished shape of the ship's hull (Illus. 9.10).
5. Sand surfaces to pre-finish condition.
6. Paint the completed hull battleship grey.

SUPERSTRUCTURE

7. Lay out and cut the various pieces of the superstructure using ¾" (19 mm) wood stock, with the exception of parts 6 and 7 which are to be ⁵⁄₁₆" (7.93 mm) thick and are supported by ½" (12.7 mm) dowel sections (Illus. 9.11).

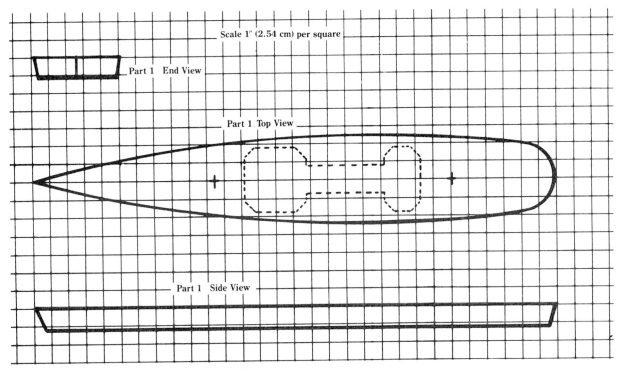

Scale 1″ (2.54 cm) per square

Part 1 End View

Part 1 Top View

Part 1 Side View

Illus. 9.9   Top, side and end views of Part 1, hull.

8. Sand all of the above pieces to pre-finish surfaces.

9. Assemble the superstructure (excluding gun turrets), beginning with Part 2 and continuing with Part 3, 4, etc. (Illus. 9.11). (Do not fasten Part 2 to the hull, Part 1, yet.) Use wood glue and finishing nails to fasten the parts together. Pre-drill nail holes to prevent splitting. Wherever possible, locate the finishing nails so that they will be covered by the next part in succession. This will minimize the number of nail holes to be filled on the finished product. Fill all exposed nail holes and sand to finish surface (Illus. 9.12).

10. The superstructure should be painted battleship gray at this time.

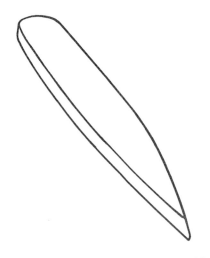

Illus. 9.10   Battleship's hull viewed upside-down to show its shape.

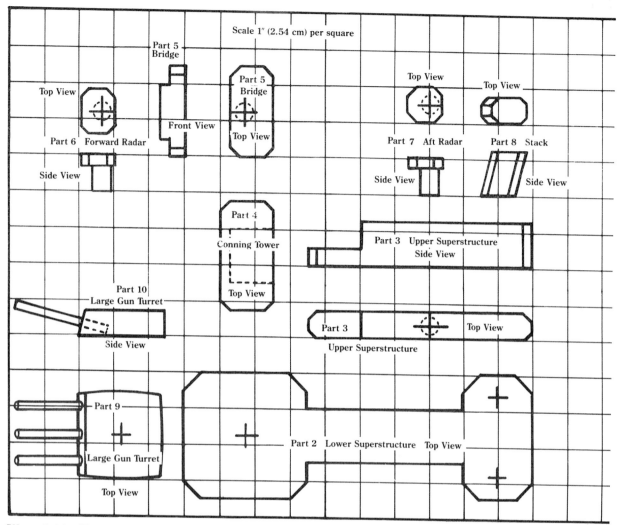

Scale 1″ (2.54 cm) per square

Part 5
Bridge

Part 5
Bridge

Front View

Top View

Top View

Top View

Top View
Part 6   Forward Radar

Part 7   Aft Radar

Part 8   Stack

Side View

Side View

Side View

Part 4

Conning Tower

Part 3   Upper Superstructure
Side View

Top View

Part 10
Large Gun Turret

Side View

Part 3

Top View

Upper Superstructure

Part 9

Large Gun Turret

Part 2   Lower Superstructure   Top View

Top View

*Illus. 9.11   Top and side views of superstructure
and gun turrets.*

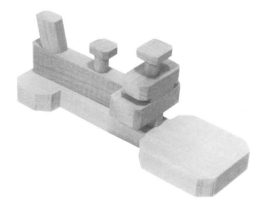

*Illus. 9.12   Battleship's superstructure, excluding
gun turret.*

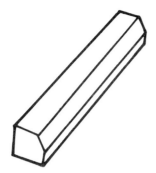

Illus. 9.13   Block of material from which small gun turrets will be cut.

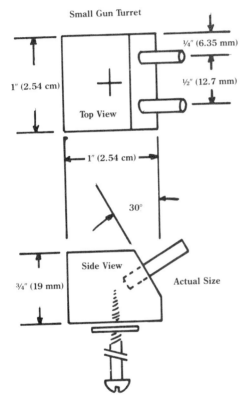

Illus. 9.14   Part 10, small gun turret.

Illus. 9.15   Small gun turret assembly.

SMALL GUN TURRETS

11. To make Part 10 cut a section of ¾" (19 mm) stock to a width of 1" (2.54 cm) and a minimum length of 7" (17.78 cm).

12. Set saw blade at an angle of 30°.

13. Trim off one corner along the length of this part, leaving approximately ¼" (6.35 mm) of the vertical side (Illus. 9.13).

14. From this section, cut off six 1" (2.54 cm)-square blocks. This will create the six small gun-turret bodies.

15. Sand these parts to prepare for finishing later.

16. On the beveled edge of the small gun-turret bodies, mark and drill two ⅛" (3.18 mm) holes. These holes should be located ¼" (6.35 mm) from each side of the turret body, ½" (12.7 mm) apart, and ¼" (6.35 mm) from the top edge. Drill perpendicular to the beveled side to a depth of ¼" (6.35 mm) (Illus. 9.14).

17. Cut 12 sections of ⅛" (3.18 mm) dowel to a length of ¾" (19 mm).

18. Sand each end of these dowel sections.

19. Apply wood glue to one end of the dowels and insert fully into holes in turret bodies (Illus. 9.15).

20. Align carefully and allow glue to dry.

21. Paint these small gun turrets battleship grey.

LARGE GUN TURRETS

22. The three large gun turrets (Part 9) will require a piece of ¾" (19 mm) stock 3" × 9" (7.62 cm × 22.87 cm).

23. Set the saw blade at an angle of 10° and cut this angle along one of the sides (Illus. 9.16).

24. Lay out the three turrets onto this piece so that the beveled edge is the front side for each.

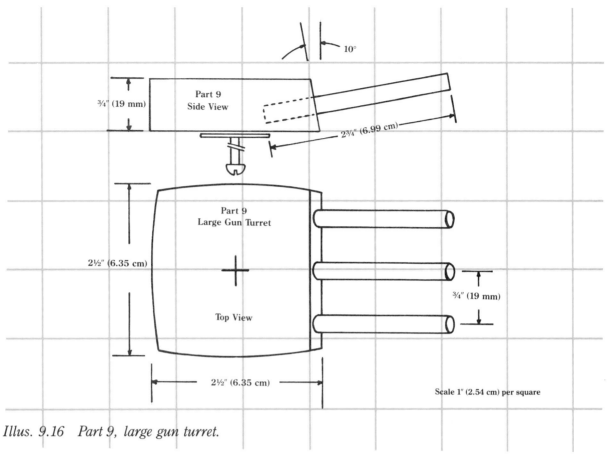

10°

¾" (19 mm)

Part 9
Side View

2¾" (6.99 cm)

Part 9
Large Gun Turret

2½" (6.35 cm)

¾" (19 mm)

Top View

2½" (6.35 cm)

Scale 1" (2.54 cm) per square

Illus. 9.16   Part 9, large gun turret.

25. Cut out the turret bodies with a bandsaw or jigsaw (Illus. 9.16).
26. Mark and drill three holes ⁹⁄₃₂" (7.14 mm) in diameter on the beveled edge of the large gun turrets. These holes should be located in the center halfway up the beveled plane with the middle hole being centered and the two outside holes being ¾" (19 mm) to either side of the center. Drill these holes ¾" (19 mm) in depth. Drill perpendicular to the beveled side.
27. Cut 9 pieces of ¼" (6.35 mm) dowel to a length of 2¾" (6.99 cm).
28. Sand each end of the dowel sections.
29. Apply wood glue to one end of each dowel and insert them fully into the holes in the front of the gun turrets.
30. Align these dowels so that they extend from the turret bodies at the same angle

Illus. 9.17   Large gun turret assembly.

and so that they are parallel to each other (Illus. 9.17). Set these assemblies aside to allow the glue to dry.
31. Paint these assemblies battleship grey.

MOUNTING TURRETS

32. At each point indicated with a cross on Parts 1 and 2 for the location of a gun turret (large or small, Illus. 9.9 and 9.11), drill a small hole. This hole should be of the size to accommodate a small diameter wood screw without friction.

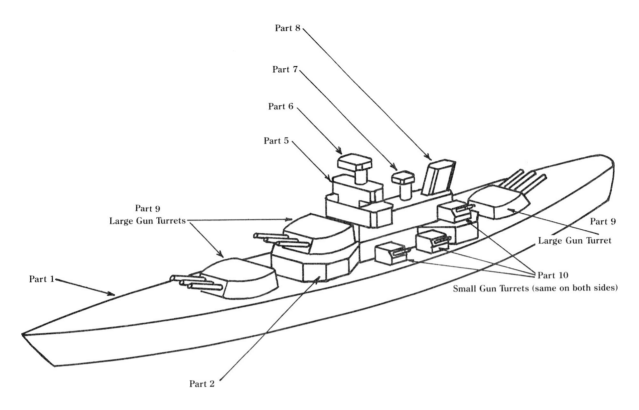

Part 8

Part 7

Part 6

Part 5

Part 9
Large Gun Turrets

Part 9
Large Gun Turret

Part 1

Part 10
Small Gun Turrets (same on both sides)

Part 2

Illus. 9.18   Battleship assembly diagram.

33. Now from the bottom side of Parts 1 and 2, drill out this hole to ⅜″ (9.52 mm) size and a depth of ¼″ (6.35 mm). This is to countersink the screw head.

34. Now place a wood screw of an appropriate length into each of these holes from the bottom side.
NOTE: The longer wood screws are to be used to mount the gun turrets (Parts 9 and 10) to the hull (Part 1).

35. Place a fender washer over the screw so that it will act as a bushing for the turret to ride on.

36. Mount the gun turret into place and tighten the screw until the turret is securely mounted, yet will still turn without binding the screw (Illus. 9.8).

FINAL ASSEMBLY

37. Locate Part 2 into position on Part 1 and secure into place with wood glue and finishing nails (Illus. 9.18).

38. Set and sink nails, fill holes and sand smooth.

PAINTING

39. Touch-up with battleship-gray paint any filled nail holes.

40. The ship's number should be painted in white on each side of the bow (front) of the hull.

41. Should you desire to christen this sea-going vessel with a name, it should be painted across the stern (rear) of the hull with small black letters. The name of the child for whom the ship was built, such as "USS Robert C. Williams," or a strong, positive personality trait such as "USS Happy Mike" make good names.

The battleship is now completed.

Submarine

Materials List

$1\frac{1}{2}''$ (3.81 cm)-thick hardwood
   stock . . . . $4\frac{1}{2}'' \times 17''$
   (11.43 cm × 43.18 cm)

$\frac{1}{2}''$ (12.7 mm)-thick hardwood
   stock . . . . $3'' \times 15''$ (7.62 cm × 38.1 cm)

$\frac{3}{8}''$ (9.52 mm)-thick hardwood
   stock . . . . $\frac{1}{2}$ board foot (1.5 meters)

Hardwood dowel:
   $\frac{1}{4}''$ (6.35 mm) diameter . . $1\frac{1}{4}''$ (3.18 cm) length
   $\frac{1}{8}''$ (3.18 mm) diameter . . $\frac{7}{8}''$ (22.2 mm) length

$1\frac{1}{2}''$ (3.81 cm) finishing nails, small box
Carpenter's glue . . . . small container
Nontoxic paint:
   Battleship grey . . . . small container
   White . . . . small amount

Illus. 9.19

Cutting List

Part 1 . . . Hull . . . . Make 1
Part 2 . . . Main Deck . . . . Make 1
Part 3 . . . Conning Tower . . . . Make 1
Part 4 . . . Forward Control Fin . . . Make 2
Part 5 . . . Rear Horizontal Control
   Fin . . . . Make 2
Part 6 . . . Rear Vertical Control
   Fin . . . . Make 1

Instructions

HULL

1. This part should be cut from the piece of wood 17" (43.18 cm) long, $4\frac{1}{2}''$ (11.43 cm) wide and $1\frac{1}{2}''$ (3.81 cm) thick.
2. Lay out the perimeter of the hull onto the wood selected for this purpose (Illus. 9.10).
3. With a bandsaw or a jigsaw, cut the entire perimeter.
4. With a $\frac{1}{2}''$ (12.7 mm) quarter-round router bit set at full depth, router the entire perimeter of both upper and lower sides of the hull.
5. Sand all surfaces to pre-finish condition.

MAIN DECK

6. The main deck is to be cut from the piece of wood $\frac{1}{2}'' \times 3'' \times 15''$ (12.7 mm × 7.62 cm × 38.1 cm).

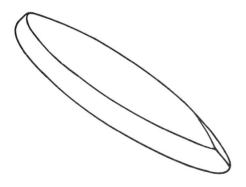

Illus. 9.20   Main deck for submarine.

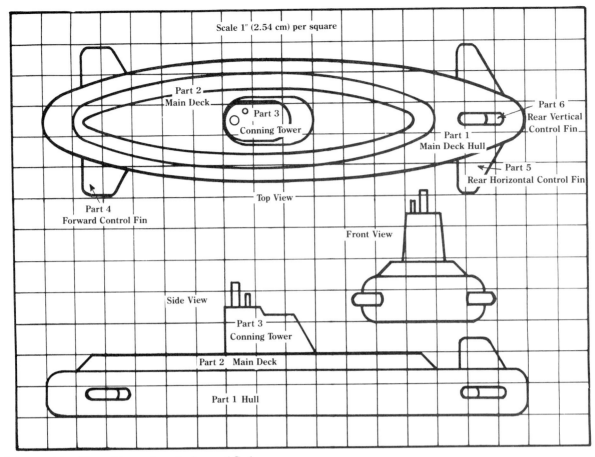

Illus. 9.21   Top, side and end views of Sub-marine.

7. Lay out this part onto the wood selected (Illus. 9.21).

8. Set your bandsaw or jigsaw for a 45° angle.

9. Cut around the perimeter so that the top is the smallest side (Illus. 9.20).

10. Sand completely.

11. Locate and secure deck into place with glue and finishing nails. Fill holes and sand smooth.

CONNING TOWER

12. The finished dimensions of the tower are 3″ (7.62 cm) long, 1½″ (3.81 cm) high and 1½″ (3.81 cm) thick.

13. Lay out and cut the side view shown in Illus. 9.22.

14. Set your bandsaw for a 5° angle and trim off both sides.

15. Set your bandsaw for a 30° angle and cut around the rear side of the tower.

16. Set bandsaw back to perpendicular position and cut around the front side.

17. Rasp all the edges to give a smooth transition between all cuts (Illus. 9.23).

18. Locate and drill two holes as indicated in Illus. 10-J to ½″ (12.7 mm) in depth.

19. Cut a ¼″ (6.35 mm) dowel section 1¼″ (3.18 cm) long.

20. Cut a ⅛″ (3.18 mm) dowel section ⅞″ (22.2 mm) long.

21. Sand these dowel sections and glue into holes (Illus. 9.22).

22. Locate and secure tower into position with glue and finishing nails.

23. Set nails, fill holes and sand smooth.

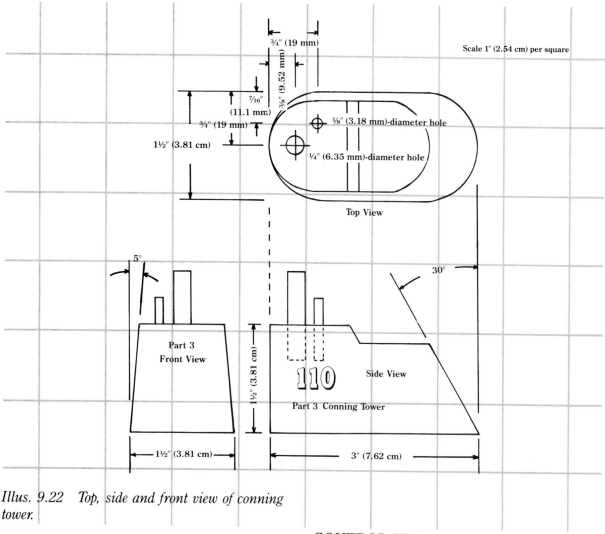

Scale 1″ (2.54 cm) per square

¾″ (19 mm)

⅜″ (9.52 mm)

⅛″ (3.18 mm)-diameter hole

⁷⁄₁₆″ (11.1 mm)

¾″ (19 mm)

¼″ (6.35 mm)-diameter hole

1½″ (3.81 cm)

Top View

5°

30°

Part 3
Front View

110   Side View

Part 3 Conning Tower

1½″ (3.81 cm)

1½″ (3.81 cm)

3″ (7.62 cm)

Illus. 9.22   Top, side and front view of conning tower.

Illus. 9.23   Conning tower for submarine.

CONTROL FINS

24. Lay out and cut the five control fins (Illus. 9.21).
25. Sand thoroughly.
26. Pre-drill all nail holes to prevent splitting.
27. Locate control fins into position and secure with glue and finishing nails (Illus. 9.21).
28. Set nails and fill holes (Illus. 9.19).

PAINTING

29. Paint the entire ship battleship grey.
30. Lay out the ship's number into position and paint white.

The Submarine is now finished and, from her underwater hiding place, is ready to protect the fleet.

Landing Ship

Materials List

¾" (19 mm)-thick hardwood
   stock . . . . 4" × 24"
   (10.16 cm ×
   60.96 cm)

⅜" (9.52 mm)-thick hardwood
   stock . . . . 4" × 24"
   (10.16 cm ×
   60.96 cm)

Dowel stock:
  ½" (12.7 mm) diameter . . ½" (12.7 mm)
   length
  ⅛" (3.18 mm) diameter . . 2" (5.08 cm)
   length
Carpenter's glue . . . . small container
Miniature lid latch 1
1½" (3.81 cm) finishing nails, small box
¾" (19 mm) wire brads . . . . . small box
Nontoxic paint:
  Battleship grey . . . . small container
  White . . . . small amount

Cutting List

Part 1 . . . Upper Hull . . . . Make 1
Part 2 . . . Lower Hull . . . . Make 1
Part 3 . . . Bow Gate . . . . Make 1
Part 4 . . . Bridge . . . . Make 1
Part 5 . . . Radar Support . . . . Make 1
Part 6 . . . Radar . . . . Make 1
Part 7 . . . Stack . . . . Make 1

Instructions

HULL

1. Choose the material that you plan to use to make Parts 1 and 2 (the two parts of the hull or body of the ship).

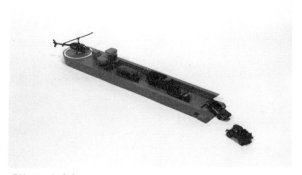

Illus. 9.24

2. Stack these two pieces together the way they will be on the finished ship.
3. Use masking tape to secure them together this way.
4. Lay out the shape of the hull on the top side of the thickest piece (Part 1) in Illus. 9.25.
5. Set your bandsaw table at a 12° angle and cut the hull shape along both sides and around the stern (rear) of the ship through both pieces of wood (Illus. 9.26).
NOTE: Do not cut across the bow (front) of the ship at this time.
6. Remove all of the masking-tape.
7. Now set your saw to cut a 45° angle and cut across the bow of each of these parts. Notice in Illus. 9.25 that Part 2 extends past the bottom of Part 1 by ½" (12.7 mm) instead of forming a continuous slope.
8. Set your bandsaw table level once again and cut out the center portion of Part 1 and the small notch at the bow end of Part 2.
9. Sand these two parts to a smooth pre-finish surface.
10. Use ¾" (19 mm) wire brads and carpenter's glue to secure Part 2 to the bottom of Part 1. Remember, at the stern end the *top* of Part 2 will extend beyond the *bottom* of Part 1 by ½" (12.7 mm).

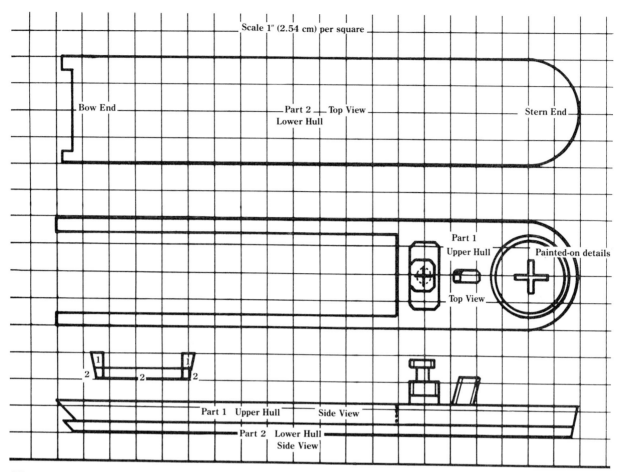

Illus. 9.25   Landing Ship diagram.

11. After the glue is dry, you can use a belt sander to shape the outside perimeter to a more uniform surface.

BOW GATE

12. Refer to Illus. 9.27 to lay out and cut the bow gate (Part 3) to shape.

13. Sand or rasp the hinge side of this part until it is rounded, so that it will operate as a hinge without binding.

14. Fit the bow gate (Part 3) into place at the bow of the ship assembly.
   NOTE: You may need to rasp or sand this part until you are satisfied with its fit.

15. When you are satisfied with the way it fits, tape it in place the way it will be when it is permanently installed.

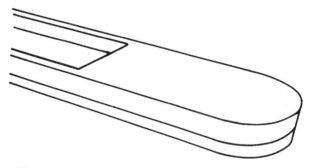

Illus. 9.26   Two-piece hull cut at 12° angle around sides and stern.

16. Now, using a ⁵⁄₃₂″ (3.97 mm) drill bit, drill the hinge-pin holes from the outside of the ship's hull through and into the bow-gate hinge. Drill to a depth of approximately ¾″ (19 mm).

17. Remove the tape.
18. Place ⅛″ (3.18 mm) dowels into these hinge-pin holes temporarily and operate the gate to check how well it functions (Illus. 9.29).
    NOTE: You may need to do some more sanding or shaping to improve its operation.
19. When you are satisfied with the bow gate's operation, glue the ⅛″ (3.18 mm) dowels in place. Be careful not to get glue between the moving parts.
20. Cut off the excess protruding dowel and sand smooth with the ship's hull.

SUPERSTRUCTURE

21. Lay out and cut to shape Parts 4, 5, 6 and 7 as shown in Illus. 9.28.

22. Sand all these parts to a smooth pre-finish surface.
23. Locate these parts in place and secure with glue and 1½″ (3.81 cm) finishing nails (Illus. 9.28 and 9.30). Pre-drill nail holes to avoid splitting. Set these nails, fill the holes and sand smooth.

PAINTING

24. Paint the entire ship battleship grey.
25. Lay out the heliport markings as shown in Illus. 9.25 and paint these markings white.
26. Install a small lid latch on one side of the bow to hold the bow gate closed.

The Landing Ship is now ready to begin its work. It can be outfitted with army trucks, tanks and other vehicles by purchasing small die-cast metal toys from the local toy store.

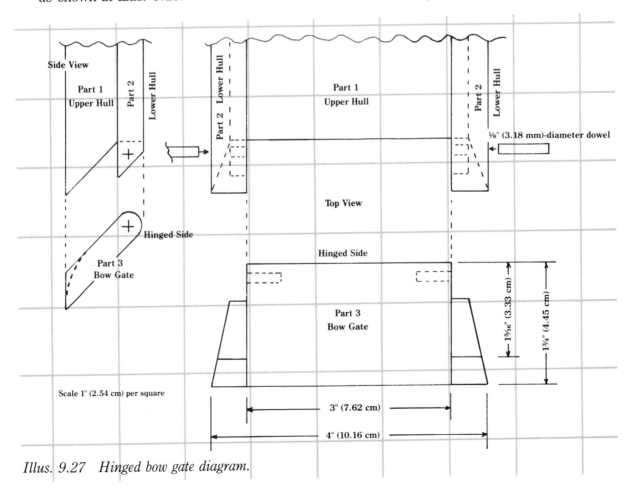

Illus. 9.27 Hinged bow gate diagram.

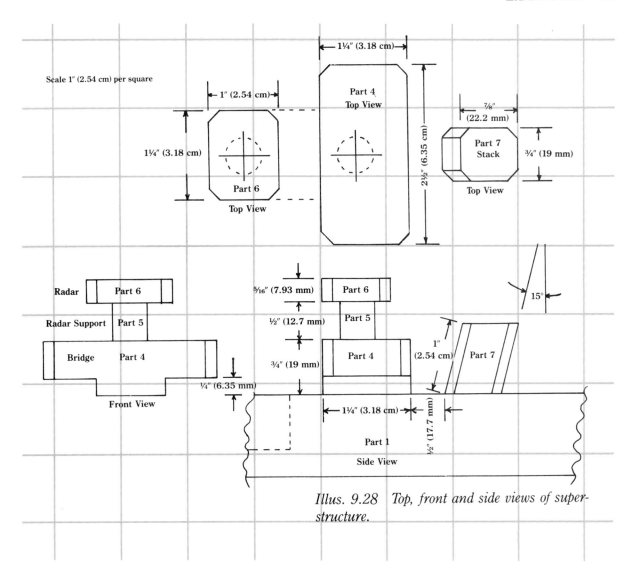

Scale 1″ (2.54 cm) per square

Part 6
Top View

Part 4
Top View

Part 7
Stack
Top View

1¼″ (3.18 cm)
1″ (2.54 cm)
1¼″ (3.18 cm)
2½″ (6.35 cm)
⅞″ (22.2 mm)
¾″ (19 mm)

Radar — Part 6
Radar Support — Part 5
Bridge — Part 4
Front View

⁵⁄₁₆″ (7.93 mm)
½″ (12.7 mm)
¾″ (19 mm)
¼″ (6.35 mm)

Part 6
Part 5
Part 4
Part 7
15°
1″ (2.54 cm)
1¼″ (3.18 cm)
½″ (17.7 mm)
Part 1
Side View

Illus. 9.28   Top, front and side views of super-structure.

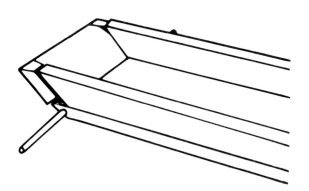
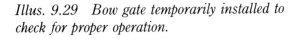

Illus. 9.29   Bow gate temporarily installed to check for proper operation.

Illus. 9.30   Installation of superstructure.

Naval Destroyer

Materials List

1" (2.54 cm)-thick hardwood, 3" × 14" (7.62 cm × 35.56 cm)

¾" (19 mm)-thick hardwood, ½ board foot (1.5 meters)

¼" (6.35 mm)-diameter dowel, 8" (20.32 cm) length

No. 8 × 1" (2.54 cm)
   roundhead woodscrews ... 2
No. 8 flat washers 2
1½" (3.81 cm) finishing nails, small box
Carpenter's glue .... small amounts
Nontoxic paint:
   Battleship grey .... small container
   White .... small amount

Illus. 9.31

Illus. 9.32   Top, side and end view of Naval Destroyer.

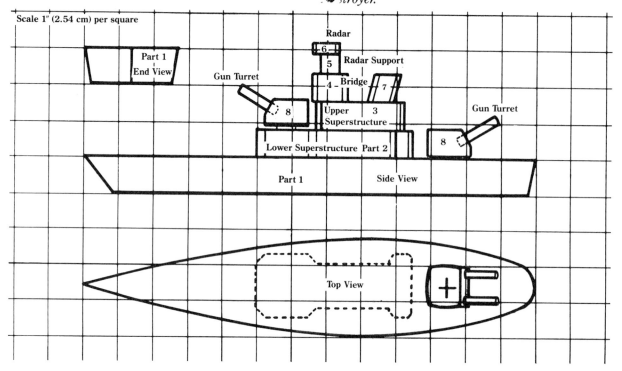

Cutting List

Part 1 ... Hull .... Make 1
Part 2 ... Lower Superstructure .. Make 1
Part 3 ... Upper Superstructure ... Make 1
Part 4 ... Bridge .... Make 1
Part 5 ... Radar Support .... Make 1
Part 6 ... Radar .... Make 1
Part 7 ... Stack .... Make 1
Part 8 ... Gun Turret .... Make 2

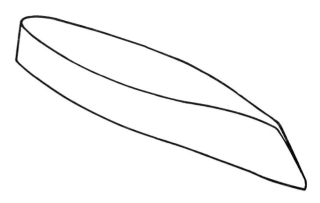

Illus. 9.33   Cut the entire perimeter of the ship's hull with your bandsaw set at 10° angle (hull shown upside down).

Instructions

HULL

1. Lay out the shape of the ship's hull (Part 1) on a piece of 1″ (2.54 cm) hardwood stock (Illus. 9.32).
2. Set your bandsaw table to cut a 10° angle.
3. Cut the entire perimeter of the ship's hull with this angle cut (Illus. 9.33).
4. Sand this part to a smooth pre-finish surface.
5. Paint the ship's hull battleship grey at this time.

SUPERSTRUCTURE

6. Lay out and cut the following parts of the superstructure from ¾″ (19 mm) stock: Parts 2, 3, 4, and 7 (Illus. 9.34).
7. Lay out and cut Part 6 from ⁵⁄₁₆″ (7.94 mm) stock.
8. Part 5 is a ½″ (12.7 mm) length of ⅜″ (9.52 mm)-diameter dowel.
9. Sand all of the above parts to a smooth pre-finish surface.
10. Assemble the parts of the superstructure as shown in Illus. 9.34 and 9.35, beginning with Part 2 and building upward. Use glue and 1½″ (3.81 cm) finishing nails. Predrill nail holes to avoid splitting. Wherever possible, locate the nail holes where they will be covered by the next part in succession.

Set all exposed nails, fill those holes, and sand smooth.

NOTE: Do not attach the superstructure to the ship's hull at this time.

11. Paint the superstructure assembly battleship grey.

GUN TURRETS

12. To make Part 8 (Illus. 9.34), cut a section of ¾″ (19 mm) stock to a width of 1¼″ (3.18 cm) and a minimum length of 3½″ (8.89 cm).
13. Set your saw blade to cut at a 30° angle.
14. Trim off one corner along the length of this piece of wood, leaving approximately ¼″ (6.35 mm) of the vertical side.
15. From this section, cut off two 1½″ (3.81 cm) blocks. This will create the two gun-turret bodies (Illus. 9.36).
16. Sand the parts well, curving each side a little for added affect (Illus. 9.34).
17. On the beveled edge of each gun turret body, mark and drill two ⁹⁄₃₂″ (7.14 mm) holes to a depth of ¼″ (6.35 mm). These holes should be spaced ¾″ (19 mm) apart, located equidistant from the center and ¼″ (6.35 mm) from the top edge of the beveled

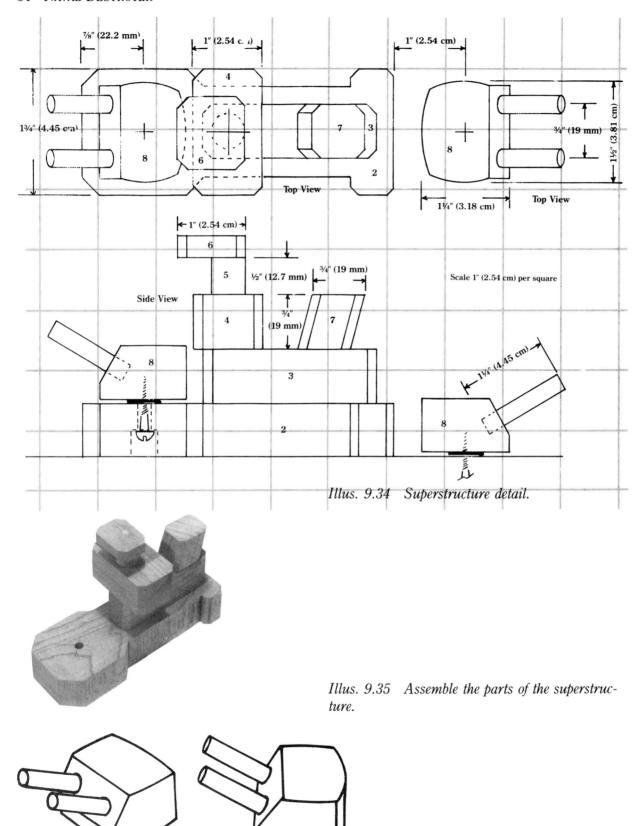

⅞" (22.2 mm)

1" (2.54 c.)

1" (2.54 cm)

4

7   3

2

8

6

Top View

1¾" (4.45 cm)

8

¾" (19 mm)

1½" (3.81 cm)

1¼" (3.18 cm)

Top View

1" (2.54 cm)

6

5

½" (12.7 mm)

¾" (19 mm)

Side View

4

¾"
(19 mm)

7

Scale 1" (2.54 cm) per square

8

3

1¼" (4.45 cm)

2

8

Illus. 9.34   Superstructure detail.

*Illus. 9.35   Assemble the parts of the superstruc-
ture.*

Illus. 9.36   Gun turret assemblies.

Illus. 9.37   Gun turrets installed.

side. Drill perpendicular to this beveled edge (Illus. 9.34).

18. Cut four sections of ¼″ (6.35 mm) dowel to a length of 1¼″ (3.18 cm).
19. Sand each end of these dowel sections.
20. Apply glue to one end of the dowels and insert fully into the holes in the turret bodies (Illus. 9.36).
21. Align the dowels carefully and allow glue to dry.
22. Paint the completed gun turrets battleship grey.

MOUNTING TURRETS

23. Mark the location point of each gun turret. One should be located on the forward end of Part 2 and the other on the aft end of Part 1 (Illus. 9.32 and 9.34).
24. Drill a small hole at each of these locations.

25. From the bottom side of each part concerned, drill out this hole to ⅜″ (9.52 mm)-diameter at a depth of ¼″ (6.35 mm). This is done to countersink the screw head of the turret mounting screw.
26. Place roundhead woodscrews into these holes from the bottom of the parts.
27. Fit a flat washer over the screws where they extend through these parts. This is to serve as a bearing for the turret to swivel upon.
28. Mount the turrets into place and tighten the screw until they are securely mounted, yet will still turn without binding the screw (Illus. 9.37).

FINAL ASSEMBLY

29. Locate the superstructure assembly into position on the ship's hull and secure in place with glue and finishing nails (Illus. 9.31).
30. Set the nails, fill the holes and sand smooth.

PAINTING

31. Touch-up any filled nail holes with battleship grey paint.
32. The ship's number should be painted in white on each side of the bow (front) of the hull.

This Naval Destroyer is now ready to join the fleet on its first exercise upon the high seas.

Chapter 10
The Play House Kitchen

The heart of every nation is its homes, and the heart of the home is its kitchen. The kitchen is where the family comes together, where love is shared, where instruction is given. It is where the family laughs together.

This chapter will endeavor to reproduce this area of the home in such a way that it can be enjoyed by your small ones in their make-believe world.

Here you will have an opportunity to build child-size versions of a refrigerator, kitchen range, sink cabinet, table and chair set and even a baby's cradle for the little dollies to sleep in.

These toys will bring hours of joy into the hearts of your little ones as they have for mine.

Play House Refrigerator

Materials List

¾" (19 mm) veneer plywood,   1 sheet
¼" (6.35 mm) veneer plywood, 1 sheet
¾" (19 mm) hardwood stock,   3 board feet (9.2 meters)

Cabinet door hinges (lip door
    type) 4
Cabinet door handles 2
Carpenter's glue . . . . small container
1¾" (4.45 cm) finishing nails, small box
Wood filler . . . . small amount
Nontoxic paint: your choice of color in small containers

Illus. 10.1

Cutting List

Part 1 . . . Side Wall . . . . Make 2
Part 2 . . . Interior Shelf . . . . Make 4
Part 3 . . . Top . . . . Make 1
Part 4 . . . Back . . . . Make 1
Part 5 . . . Toe Board . . . . Make 1

Part 6 . . . Upper Door . . . . Make 1
Part 7 . . . Lower Door . . . . Make 1
Part 8 . . . Face Frame Side Rail . . Make 2
Part 9 . . . Face Frame Cross Rail, Make 3

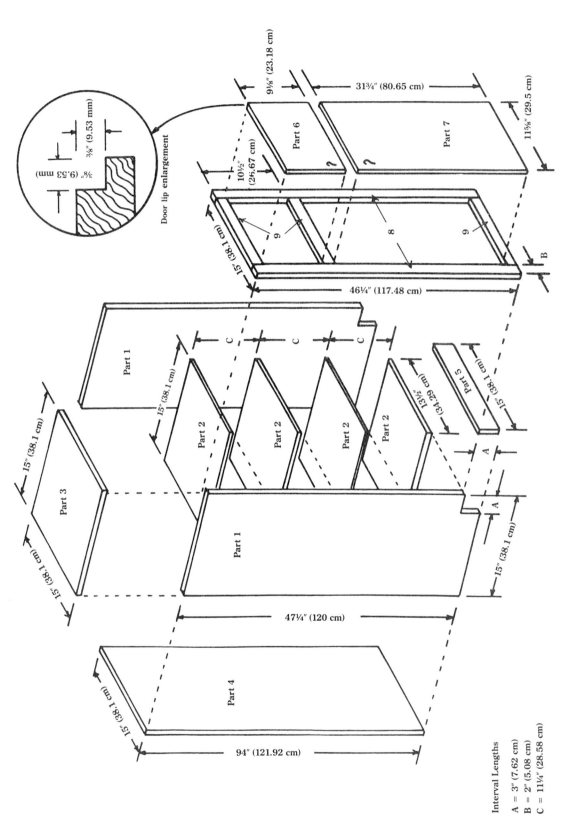

Illus. 10.2   *Play House Refrigerator diagram.*

9⅛" (23.18 cm)

31¾" (80.65 cm)

11⅝" (29.5 cm)

⅜" (9.53 mm)

⅜" (9.53 mm)

Door lip enlargement

Part 6

Part 7

10½" (26.67 cm)

15" (38.1 cm)

46¼" (117.48 cm)

9   8   9

B

Part 1

C   C   C

15" (38.1 cm)

13½" (34.29 cm)

Part 5

15" (38.1 cm)

Part 2   Part 2   Part 2   Part 2

Part 3

15" (38.1 cm)

15" (38.1 cm)

Part 1

A

A

15" (38.1 cm)

47¼" (120 cm)

Part 4

15" (38.1 cm)

94" (121.92 cm)

Interval Lengths

A = 3" (7.62 cm)

B = 2" (5.08 cm)

C = 11¼" (28.58 cm)

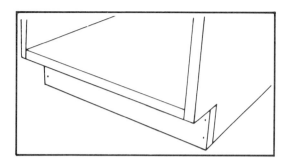

Illus. 10.3   Installation of shelves and toe board.

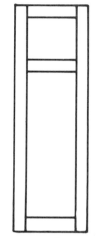

Illus. 10.4   Layout and assembly of face frame.

Illus. 10.5   Installation of face frame.

Instructions

LAYOUT

1. Lay out and cut two side walls (Part 1), four shelves (Part 2), and one top (Part 3) from ¾″ (19 mm) veneer plywood (Illus. 10.2). NOTE: Part 1 has a 3″ × 3″ (7.62 cm × 7.62 cm) cutout at the lower front corner. This is a toe cutout.

2. Lay out and cut the back (Part 4) from ¼″ (6.35 mm) plywood (Illus. 10.2).

3. Sand the parts well to prepare for assembly.

ASSEMBLY

4. Beginning at the toe cutout, measure and mark the four shelf locations at intervals of 11¼″ (28.58 cm) along the front edge of each side (Part 1).

5. Using a small framing square to insure accuracy, continue these marks across the inside of each side.

6. Now use carpenter's glue and finishing nails to attach the shelves (Part 2) to one side at a time. The shelves should be aligned so that their bottom edge is located on the marks made in Step 5 (Illus. 10.3).

7. Install the top (Part 3) and the back (Part 4) with glue and finishing nails.

8. The toe board (Part 5) can now be cut from ¾″ (19 mm) hardwood stock. This board should measure 3″ × 15″ (7.62 cm × 38.1 cm).

9. Install the toe board into the toe cutout and secure with glue and finishing nails (Illus. 10.3).

FACE FRAME

10. The face frame is made of five pieces of ¾″ (19 mm) hardwood. All five pieces are cut to a width of 2″ (5.08 cm). The side rails (Part 8) are 46¼″ (117.5 cm) long and the

Illus. 10.6   Cut a lip around the entire perimeter of the back side of each door. Use lip type cabinet hinges to hang the door.

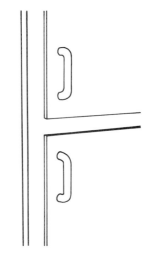

Illus. 10.7   Installation of cabinet door handles.

cross rails (Part 9) are 11″ (29.5 cm) long. Cut these parts and sand for assembly.

11. Lay out the face frame on your workbench by locating a cross rail (Part 9) flush with each end of each side rail (Part 8) and the third cross rail (Part 9) 11¼″ (28.58 cm) down from the top of each side rail (Illus. 10.4).

NOTE: The top of the middle cross-member should be flush with the top of the top shelf when the assembly is completed.

12. Mark and assemble the face frame in this configuration.

NOTE: You can use whatever jointing method you prefer for this assembly. Dowel and glue joints work well and are simple and easy to do.

13. The face frame can now be installed to the cabinet assembly using glue and finishing nails (Illus. 10.5).

FINISHING

14. At this time, all nails should be counterset and the nail holes filled with wood filler.

15. The entire cabinet assembly can now be finish-sanded to prepare it for final finishing.

16. The doors (Parts 6 and 7) can now be cut from ¾″ (19 mm) veneer plywood (Illus. 10.2).

17. Cut a ⅜″ × ⅜″ (9.53 mm × 9.53 mm) lip from the back side of each door around the entire perimeter.

18. Sand these parts well to prepare them for installation.

19. Use two cabinet door hinges to install each of these doors (Illus. 10.6).

20. Install a cabinet door handle on each door. Locate these handles near the cross member on the nonhinged side of the door (Illus. 10.7).

21. The entire project can now be painted with a nontoxic paint of your color choice.

This completes the Play House Refrigerator.

Play House Range

Materials List

¾" (19 mm) veneer plywood,   ½ sheet
¼" (6.35 mm) veneer plywood, ¼ sheet
¾" (19 mm) hardwood stock,   2½ board feet
Cabinet door hinges (lip door
    type) 2
Cabinet door handle 1
Lid support .... 1 set
1½" (3.81 cm)-diameter
    wooden toy wheels 10
¼" (6.35 mm) dowel .... 15" (38.1 cm)
Carpenter's glue .... small container
1¾" (4.45 cm) finishing nails, small box
Wood filler .... small amount
Nontoxic paint: your color choice in small
containers

Illus. 10.8

Cutting List

Part 1 ... Side Wall .... *Make 2*
Part 2 ... Interior Shelf .... *Make 1*
Part 3 ... Top .... *Make 1*
Part 4 ... Back .... *Make 1*
Part 5 ... Door .... *Make 1*
Part 6 ... Toe Board .... *Make 1*
Part 7 ... Back Frame Vertical
             Support .... *Make 2*
Part 8 ... Back Frame Crosspiece, *Make 1*
Part 9 ... Face Frame Side Rail .. *Make 2*
Part 10 .. Face Frame Upper Cross
             Rail .... *Make 1*
Part 11 .. Face Frame Lower Cross
             Rail .... *Make 1*

Instructions

LAYOUT

1. Lay out and cut two side walls (Part 1), one shelf (Part 2), and one top (Part 3) from ¾" (19 mm) veneer plywood (Illus. 10.9).
   NOTE: Part 1 has a 3" × 3" (7.62 cm × 7.62 cm) cutout at the lower front corner. This is a toe cutout.
2. Lay out and cut the back (Part 4) from ¼" (6.35 mm) veneer plywood (Illus. 10.9).
3. Sand these parts well to prepare them for assembly.

TOE KICK

4. Using carpenter's glue and finishing nails, attach the shelf (Part 2) to the side walls (Part 1) one side at a time.
   NOTE: The bottom of the shelf should be installed flush with the horizontal cut of the toe cutout (Illus. 10.10).
5. Install the top (Part 3) and the back (Part 4) with glue and finishing nails.
   NOTE: The back (Part 4) will extend above the top by 4" (10.16 cm).

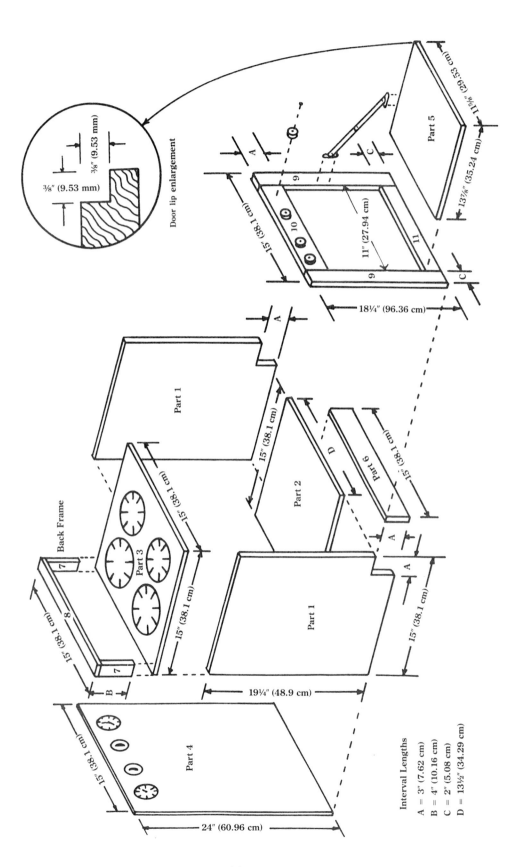

3/8" (9.53 mm)

3/8" (9.53 mm)

Door lip enlargement

Part 5

11 5/8" (29.53 cm)

13 7/8" (35.24 cm)

A

C

C

9

10

9

11

11" (27.94 cm)

15" (38.1 cm)

18 1/4" (96.36 cm)

Part 1

A

15" (38.1 cm)

15" (38.1 cm)

Part 2

D

Part 6

15" (38.1 cm)

A

A

Part 1

15" (38.1 cm)

Back Frame

7

Part 3

7

8

15" (38.1 cm)

15" (38.1 cm)

15" (38.1 cm)

B

19 1/4" (48.9 cm)

Part 4

15" (38.1 cm)

24" (60.96 cm)

Interval Lengths

A = 3" (7.62 cm)
B = 4" (10.16 cm)
C = 2" (5.08 cm)
D = 13 1/2" (34.29 cm)

Illus. 10.9 Play House Range diagram.

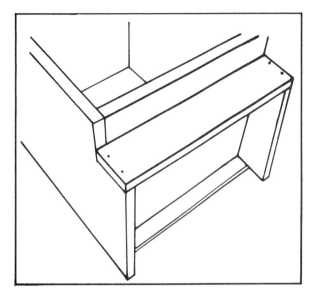

Illus. 10.10   Installation of shelf and toe board.

6. The toe board (Part 6) can now be cut from ¾″ (19 mm) hardwood stock. This part should measure 3″ × 15″ (7.62 cm × 38.1 cm).

7. Install the toe board (Part 6) into the cutout and secure with glue and finishing nails (Illus. 10.10).

FACE FRAME

8. The face frame is made of four pieces cut from ¾″ (19 mm) hardwood stock (Illus. 10.9). The upper cross rail (Part 10) is 3″ × 11″ (7.62 cm × 27.94 cm). The lower cross rail (Part 11) measures 2″ × 11″ (5.08 cm × 27.94 cm). Both side rails (Part 9) are 2″ × 18¼″ (5.08 cm × 46.36 cm). Cut these parts and sand for assembly.

9. Lay out the face frame on your workbench by locating the cross members (Parts 10 and 11) flush with the top and bottom of the side rails (Part 9).

10. Mark and assemble the face frame in this configuration.

NOTE: You can use whatever jointing method you prefer for this assembly. Dowel and glue joints work quite well and are simple and easy to do.

11. Install the face frame to the front of the cabinet assembly with glue and finishing nails (Illus. 10.11).

12. Construct the back frame from two back frame vertical supports (Part 7) of ¾″ (19 mm) stock cut 2″ × 3¼″ (5.08 cm × 8.26 cm), and one back frame crosspiece (Part 8) cut 2″ × 15″ (5.08 cm × 38.1 cm). Assemble as shown in Illus. 10.9.

13. Install with glue and finishing nails.

14. Fill nail holes and finish-sand.

BURNERS AND DIALS

15. The top range burners are cut from ¼″ (6.35 mm) plywood. The two front burners are 5″ (12.7 cm) in diameter and the back burners are 6″ (15.24 cm) in diameter.

16. Locate these burners in place symmetrically on the top and glue in place (Illus. 10.12).

Illus. 10.11   Installation of face frame.

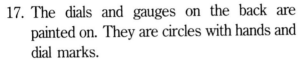

Illus. 10.12   Place burners symmetrically on the top and glue in place.

Illus. 10.13   Install the knobs.

17. The dials and gauges on the back are painted on. They are circles with hands and dial marks.
18. The knobs on the face frame at the front (on Part 10, the upper cross rail) are 1½" (3.81 cm) toy wheels mounted on ¼" (6.35 mm) dowels.
    NOTE: The ¼" (6.35 mm) dowels are inserted through ⁹⁄₃₂" (7.14 mm) holes and have another wheel glued on the back side as a retainer (Illus. 10.13).

DOOR

19. The door is cut from ¾" (19 mm) veneer plywood and has a ⅜" × ⅜" (9.53 mm × 9.53 mm) lip cut around the entire perimeter of the inside edge.
20. Mount the door with two cabinet door lip-type hinges along the bottom side.
21. Install a set of lid supports on the door so that it will open to a level position (Illus. 10.14).
22. Install one cabinet door handle on the front of the door near the top edge at the center.
23. Paint the toy range with nontoxic paint of your color choice.

The Play House Range is now complete.

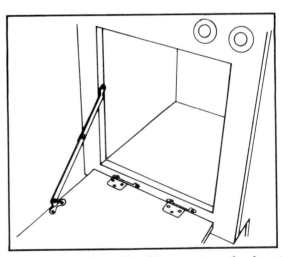

Illus. 10.14   Install a lid support on the door to allow it to open to a level position.

Play House Kitchen Sink

Materials List

¾″ (19 mm) veneer plywood,   ½ sheet
¼″ (6.35 mm) veneer plywood, ¼ sheet
¾″ (19 mm) hardwood stock,   3 board feet
                             (9.14 meters)

Cabinet door hinges (lip door
    type) 4
Cabinet door handle 2
Small plastic dishpan, 12″
    (30.48 cm) maximum
    diameter 1
2″ (5.08 cm)-diameter wooden
    toy wheels 2
Carpenter's glue . . . . small container
1¾″ (4.45 cm) finishing nails, small box
Wood filler . . . . small amount
Nontoxic paint: your color choice in small
containers

Cutting List

Part 1 . . . Side Wall . . . . Make 2
Part 2 . . . Interior Shelf . . . . Make 1
Part 3 . . . Top . . . . Make 1
Part 4 . . . Back . . . . Make 1
Part 5 . . . Door . . . . Make 2
Part 6 . . . Toe Board . . . . Make 1
Part 7 . . . Back Frame Cross Rail, Make 1
Part 8 . . . Back Frame Vertical
                Supports . . . . Make 2
Part 9 . . . Face Frame Side Rail . . Make 2
Part 10 . . Face Frame Center Rail, Make 1
Part 11 . . Face Frame Upper Cross
                Rail . . . . Make 1
Part 12 . . Face Frame Lower Cross
                Rail . . . . Make 1
Part 13 . . Faucet Base . . . . Make 1
Part 14 . . Faucet Spout . . . . Make 1

Illus. 10.15

Instructions

LAYOUT

1. Lay out and cut two side walls (Part 1), one shelf (Part 2), and one top (Part 3) from ¾″ (19 mm) veneer plywood (Illus. 10.16).
    NOTE: Part 1 has a 3″ × 3″ (7.62 cm × 7.62 cm) cutout at the lower front corner. This is a toe cutout.

2. Lay out and cut the back (Part 4) from ¼″ (6.35 mm) veneer plywood (Illus. 10.16).

3. Sand these parts to prepare them for assembly.

CABINET

4. Use carpenter's glue and finishing nails and install the shelf (Part 2) to the side walls (Part 1) one side at a time.
    NOTE: The bottom of the shelf should be flush with the horizontal cut of the toe cutout.

5. Install the top (Part 3) and the back (Part 4) with glue and finishing nails.
    NOTE: The back (Part 4) will extend above the top by 4″ (10.16 cm).

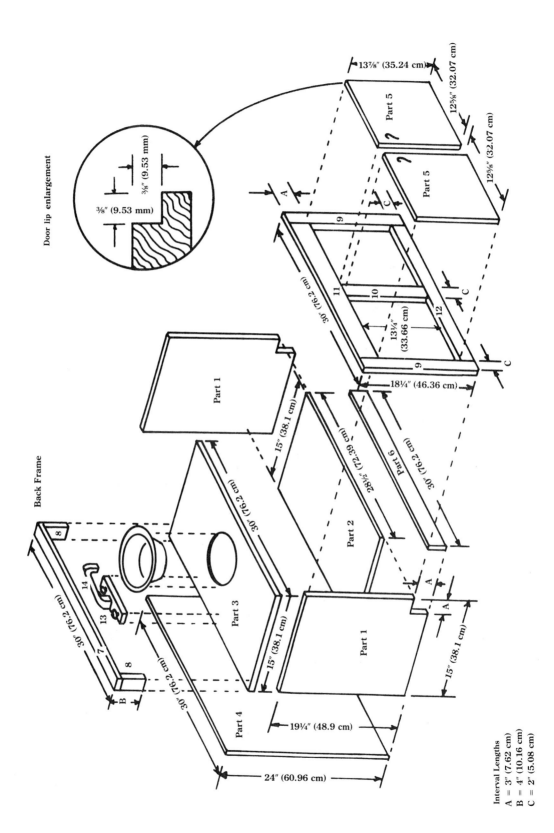

Door lip enlargement

⅜" (9.53 mm)

⅜" (9.53 mm)

Part 5

13⅞" (35.24 cm)

12⅝" (32.07 cm)

12⅝" (32.07 cm)

Part 5

12⅝" (32.07 cm)

A

C

9

11

10

12

13¼" (33.66 cm)

C

C

30" (76.2 cm)

9

18¼" (46.36 cm)

Part 1

15" (38.1 cm)

28½" (72.39 cm)

30" (76.2 cm)

Part 6

30" (76.2 cm)

Part 2

Back Frame

8

14

13

7

8

B

30" (76.2 cm)

30" (76.2 cm)

Part 3

Part 4

15" (38.1 cm)

Part 1

A

A

15" (38.1 cm)

19¼" (48.9 cm)

24" (60.96 cm)

Interval Lengths
A = 3" (7.62 cm)
B = 4" (10.16 cm)
C = 2" (5.08 cm)

Illus. 10.16 Play House Kitchen Sink diagram.

6. Cut the toe board (Part 6) from ¾″ (19 mm) hardwood stock. It should measure 3″ × 15″ (7.62 cm × 38.1 cm).

7. Install the toe board (Part 6) with glue and finishing nails into the toe cutout (Illus. 10.16).

FACE FRAME

8. The face frame parts are all 2″ (5.08 cm) wide except for the upper cross rail (Part 11) which is 3″ (7.62 cm) wide. Both cross rails (Parts 11 and 12) are 26″ (66.04 cm) long. The two side rails (Part 9) are 18¼″ (46.36 cm) long and the center rail (Part 10) is 13¼″ (33.66 cm) long. Cut these five parts and sand for assembly.

9. Lay out the face frame on your workbench in the configuration in which it will be assembled (Illus. 10.16).

10. Mark and assemble the face frame.
NOTE: You can use whatever jointing method you prefer for this assembly. Dowel and glue joints are quite effective and are easy and simple to do.

11. Install the face frame with glue and finishing nails (Illus. 10.17).

12. Construct the back frame vertical supports (Part 8) from two pieces of ¾″ (19 mm) hardwood stock cut to 2″ × 3¼″ (5.08 cm × 8.26 cm), and one back frame cross rail (Part 7) cut to 2″ × 30″ (5.08 cm × 76.2 cm). Assemble as shown in Illus 10.16.

13. Install the back frame with glue and finishing nails.

14. Fill all the nail holes and finish-sand.

FAUCETS AND SINK

15. Illus. 10.20 shows the size of the faucet parts. These parts are cut from ¾″ (19 mm) hardwood stock. The two faucet handles are 2″ (5.08 cm)-diameter toy wheels.

16. Cut the faucet parts to shape and assemble at this time. Mount the handles on ¼″ (6.35 mm) dowel sections glued into the base part (Illus. 10.18).

17. The sink in this cabinet is simply a plastic dishpan. Lay out a cutting mark centered on the cabinet top that will conform to the size and shape of the sink that you plan to use.
NOTE: This mark should be laid out so that when the hole is cut, the plastic dishpan will drop through the hole only as far as its lip ring.

18. Cut out and install the sink (Illus. 10.19).

19. Install the faucet behind the sink with glue and finishing nails.

Illus. 10.17   Installation of face frame.

Illus. 10.18   Faucet assembly.

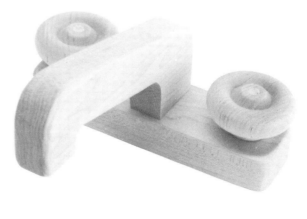

DOORS

20. Lay out and cut the cabinet doors (Part 5) from ¾″ (19 mm) veneer plywood.
21. Lip-cut the perimeter of both doors with a ⅜″ × ⅜″ (9.53 mm × 9.53 mm) lip.
22. Install these doors with lip-type cabinet door hinges.
23. Install cabinet door handles.
24. Finish the sink cabinet with nontoxic paint of your color choice.

The Play House Kitchen Sink is now ready for service with the other kitchen toys.

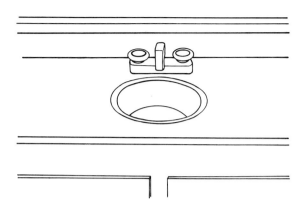

Illus. 10.19   Install a small plastic dish pan as a sink.

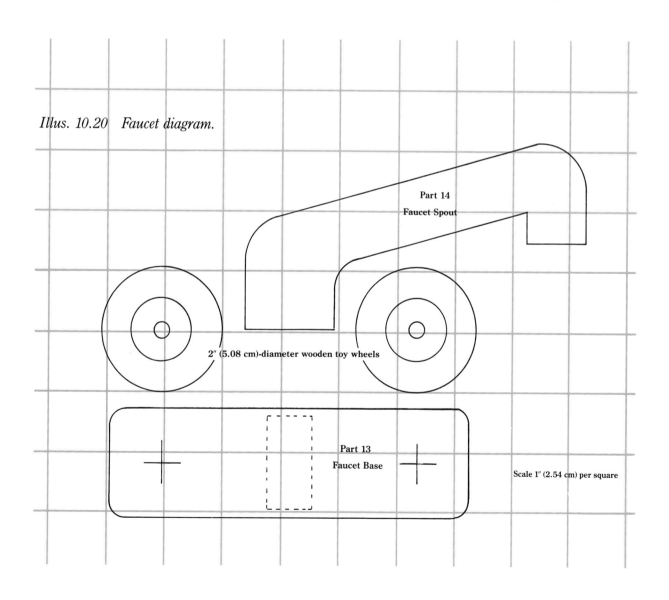

Illus. 10.20   Faucet diagram.

Part 14
Faucet Spout

2″ (5.08 cm)-diameter wooden toy wheels

Part 13
Faucet Base

Scale 1″ (2.54 cm) per square

Little Table

Materials List

¾″ (19 mm) veneer plywood,	½ sheet
¾″ (19 mm) hardwood	3½ board feet (10.7 meters)
Carpenter's glue	small amount
1½″ (3.81 cm) finishing nails,	small box
Wood filler	small amount
Nontoxic paint or varnish . . .	medium-sized containers

Cutting List

Part 1 . . . *Table Top* . . . . *Make 1*
Part 2 . . . *Top Frame Crosspiece* . . *Make 2*
Part 3 . . . *Top Frame* . . . . *Make 2*
Part 4 . . . *Leg Support Frame* . . . . *Make 4*
Part 5 . . . *Large Leg Side* . . . . *Make 4*
Part 6 . . . *Small Leg Side* . . . . *Make 4*

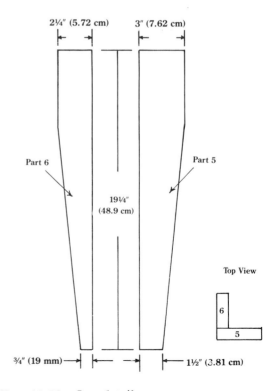

Illus. 10.21

Instructions

TOP

1. Begin the table top (Part 1) with a piece of ¾″ (19 mm) veneer plywood that is 36″ (91.44 cm) square. Select the material you

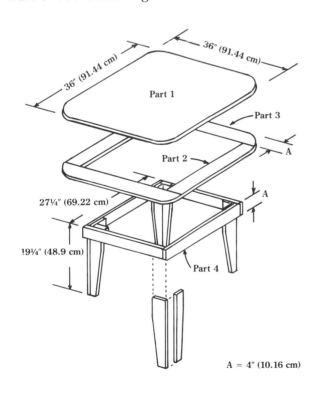

Illus. 10.22 Little Table diagram.

Illus. 10.23 Leg detail.

plan to use for the table top and cut to size (Illus. 10.22). Do not radius the corners at this time.

2. Place the table top (Part 1) face down upon your workbench.

3. Cut two each of Parts 2 and 3 from ¾″ (19 mm) veneer plywood. Part 2 will be 28″ (71.12 cm) long and Part 3 will be 36″ (91.44 cm) long.

4. Place these parts into position around the perimeter of the inverted table top (Part 1) and secure in place with glue and finishing nails (Illus. 10.24).

5. Radius the corners of the top assembly to a 4″ (10.16 cm) radius.

6. Finish-sand the top assembly.

7. Cut four of Part 4. This part measures 4″ × 27¼″ (10.16 cm × 69.22 cm).

8. Assemble these parts into a square with glue and finishing nails.
   NOTE: Overlap the ends so that the finished square is 28″ (71.12 cm) on all sides.

LEGS

9. Lay out and cut the eight parts to the table legs as shown in Illus. 10.23.

10. Assemble the parts with glue and finishing nails (Illus. 10.23 insert).

Illus. 10.24   Installation of tabletop doublers around the bottom side of the table top.

ASSEMBLY

11. Install the leg assemblies inside the corners of the table-frame assembly with glue and finishing nails (Illus. 10.25 and 10.26).

12. Fit the top assembly in place on the leg-frame assembly. The leg-frame assembly should fit into the 28″ (71.12 cm)-square depression on the bottom side of the top assembly.

13. Secure the top assembly in place with glue and finishing nails.

14. Fill all the nail holes and finish-sand the entire project.

15. Using nontoxic paint or varnish, finish the table as desired.

The Little Table is now complete.

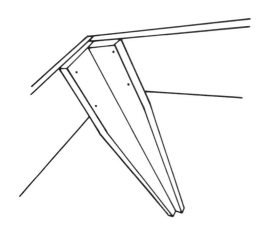

Illus. 10.25   Assembly of legs.

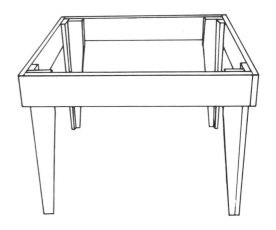

Illus. 10.26   Installation of legs.

Little Chair

Materials List

¾" (19 mm) veneer plywood,   ¼ sheet
Carpenter's glue . . . . small amount
Wood filler . . . . small amount
1¾" (4.45 cm) finishing nails, small box
Nontoxic varnish or paint . . . small amount

Cutting List

Part 1 . . . Chair Side . . . . Make 2
Part 2 . . . Seat Bottom . . . . Make 1
Part 3 . . . Seat Back . . . . Make 1
Part 4 . . . Brace . . . . Make 1

Illus. 10.27

Instructions

1. Lay out and cut to shape two of Part 1 and one each of Parts 2 and 3 from ¾" (19 mm) veneer plywood (Illus. 10.28).
2. Cut a 3" × 12" (7.62 cm × 30.48 cm) brace (Part 4) from ¾" (19 mm) veneer plywood.
3. Sand all of the parts well to prepare them for assembly.
4. Using the location marks shown on Illus. 10.28, locate and install the seat (Part 2), the back (Part 3) and the brace (Part 4), attaching them to one side at a time (Illus. 10.27). This assembly is to be done with glue and finishing nails.
5. Fill all nail holes and finish-sand the entire chair.
6. Use nontoxic varnish or paint to finish the project as desired.

The Little Chair is now ready to join the Little Table and the other kitchen toys.

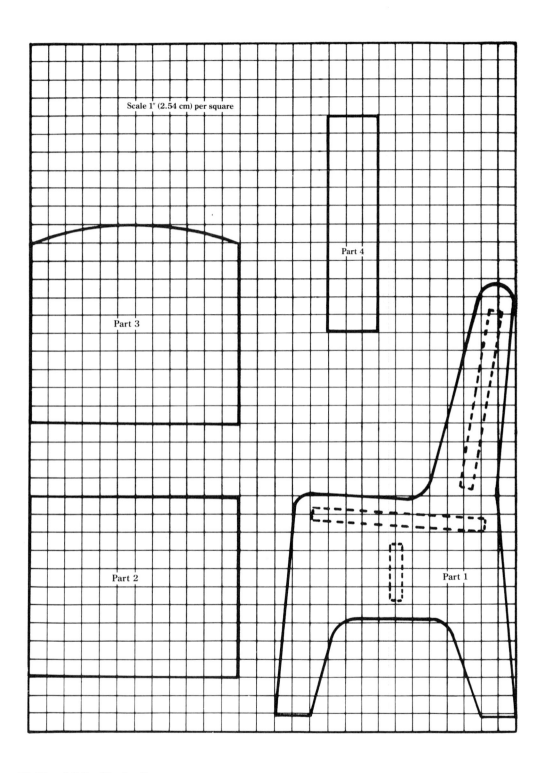

Scale 1″ (2.54 cm) per square

Part 4

Part 3

Part 2

Part 1

Illus. 10.28   Little Chair diagram.

Doll Cradle

Materials List

¾" (19 mm) veneer plywood,   *¼ sheet*
Carpenter's glue . . . . *small amount*
Wood filler . . . . *small amount*
1¾" (4.45 cm) finishing nails, *small box*
Nontoxic varnish or paint . . . *small containers*

Cutting List

Part 1   . . . Side . . . . Make 2
Part 2   . . . Head Board . . . . Make 1
Part 3   . . . Foot Board . . . . Make 1
Part 4   . . . Bottom . . . . Make 1

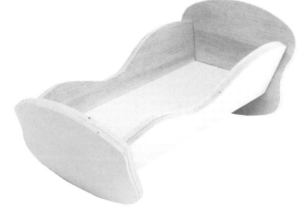

Illus. 10.29

Instructions

1. Lay out and cut to shape two of Part 1 and one each of Parts 2, 3 and 4 from ¾" (19 mm) veneer plywood (Illus. 10.30, 10.31 and 10.32).
2. Sand all these parts well.
3. Using glue and finishing nails, attach the sides (Part 1) to the bottom (Part 4) (Illus. 10.33).
4. Referring to the location marks on Illus. 10.32, install the ends (Parts 2 and 3) to the center assembly with glue and finishing nails (Illus. 10.29).
   NOTE: Make sure the center assembly is level when this assembly is done.
5. Fill all the nail holes and finish-sand the entire project.
6. Varnish or paint the cradle now to bring it to the desired finish. Use nontoxic material.

The Doll Cradle is now finished.

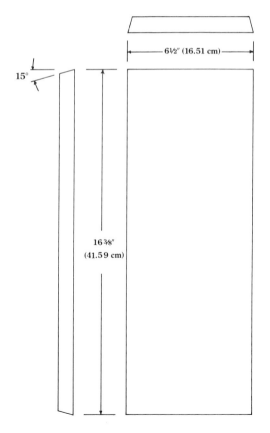

Illus. 10.30   *Top, side and end view of Part 4.*

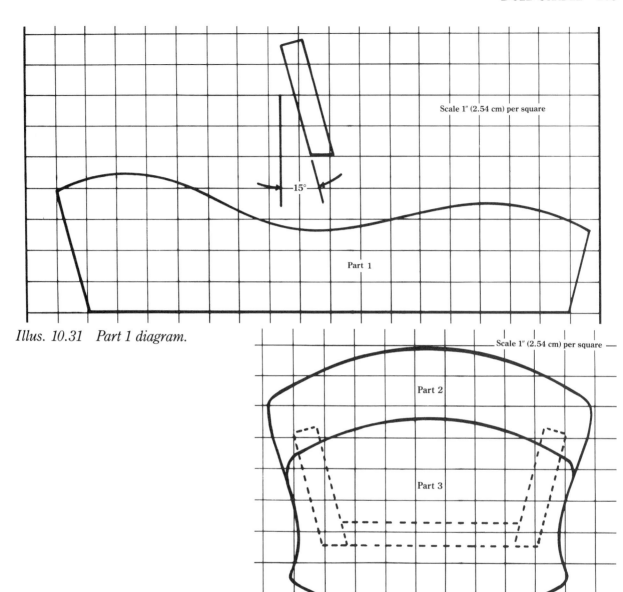

Scale 1″ (2.54 cm) per square

15°

Part 1

Illus. 10.31   Part 1 diagram.

Scale 1″ (2.54 cm) per square

Part 2

Part 3

Illus. 10.32   Doll Cradle diagram, end view.

Illus. 10.33   Install cradle sides to bottom.

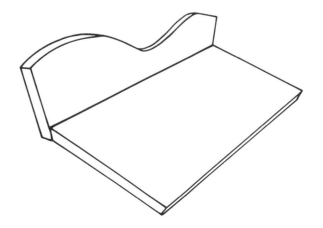

Chapter 11
Heavy Construction Toys

The machines represented here in this chapter are mechanical monsters. Their size alone sets them apart from the everyday machines that we are accustomed to. The sound of their tremendously powerful engines and the sight of diesel smoke blasting from their exhaust pipes cause our hearts to leap in pure excitement. We watch mountains literally crumble before the cutting edge of their blades. We watch valley streams become lakes because of the dams erected by these magnificent mechanical marvels.

As you build the heavy construction toys in this chapter, let your mind go back to your childhood when machines like these caused your heart to pound in excitement. Share that feeling with the child you have in mind while building these toys.

Bulldozer

Materials List

$1\frac{3}{4}$" (4.45 cm)-thick hardwood, 5" × 15" (12.7 cm × 38.1 cm)
$\frac{3}{4}$" (19 mm)-thick hardwood, 5" × 10" (12.7 cm × 25.4 cm)
Hardwood dowel:
   1" (2.54 cm) diameter .... 4" (10.16 cm)
   $\frac{1}{4}$" (6.35 mm) diameter .. 12" (30.48 cm)
No. 8 $1\frac{1}{2}$" (3.81 cm)
   roundhead woodscrews ... 2
No. 8 flat washers 2
Carpenter's glue .... small container
$1\frac{3}{4}$" (4.45 cm) finishing nails, small box
$2\frac{1}{4}$" (5.72 cm) finishing nails, small box
$\frac{3}{4}$" (19 mm) wire brads .... small box
Nontoxic paint: your color choice in small container

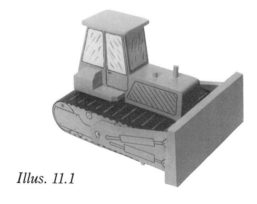

Illus. 11.1

Cutting List

Part 1 ... Body .... Make 1
Part 2 ... Top .... Make 1
Part 3 ... Track Assembly .... Make 2
Part 4 ... Blade Support .... Make 2
Part 5 ... Fuel Tank .... Make 2
Part 6 ... Blade .... Make 1

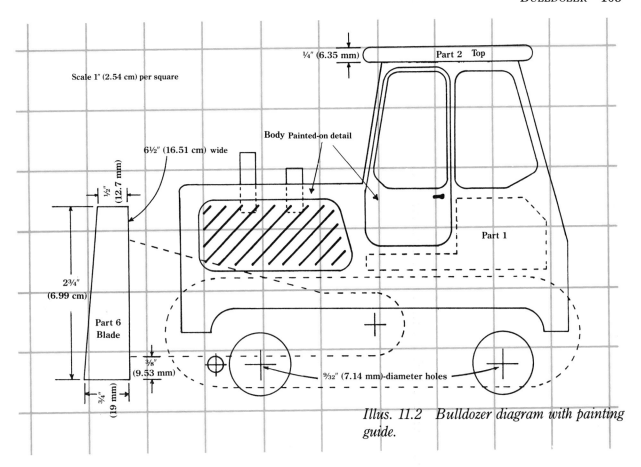

Illus. 11.2 Bulldozer diagram with painting guide.

Instructions

LAYOUT

1. Lay out and cut to shape one body (Part 1) and two each of the track assemblies (Part 3) from 1¾" (4.45 cm) hardwood stock (Illus. 11.2, 11.3 and 11.4).

2. Lay out and cut to shape the top (Part 2), bulldozer blade (Part 6), two of the bulldozer blade supports (Part 4) and the two fuel tanks (Part 5) from ¾" (19 mm) hardwood stock (Illus. 11.3 and 11.8).

3. Sand all the parts well to prepare them for assembly.

4. Locate and drill the two holes in the top of the engine area on Part 1. Use a ¼" (6.35 mm)-diameter drill bit and drill to a depth of ½" (12.7 mm).

5. Cut two pieces of ¼" (6.35 mm) dowel. One piece should be 1" (2.54 cm) and the other should be ¾" (19 mm) in length.

6. Sand the dowel sections and glue them fully into the holes at the top of the engine area on Part 1 (Illus. 11.2 and 11.4).

PAINTING

7. You will find it easier to paint the markings on the various parts prior to assembly. At this time all of the parts should be painted with nontoxic paint. A safety-yellow color is popular for this type of equipment.

8. Now paint the markings on the various parts with black paint.
NOTE: The windows should be painted white with silver slashing marks to imitate the appearance of glass.

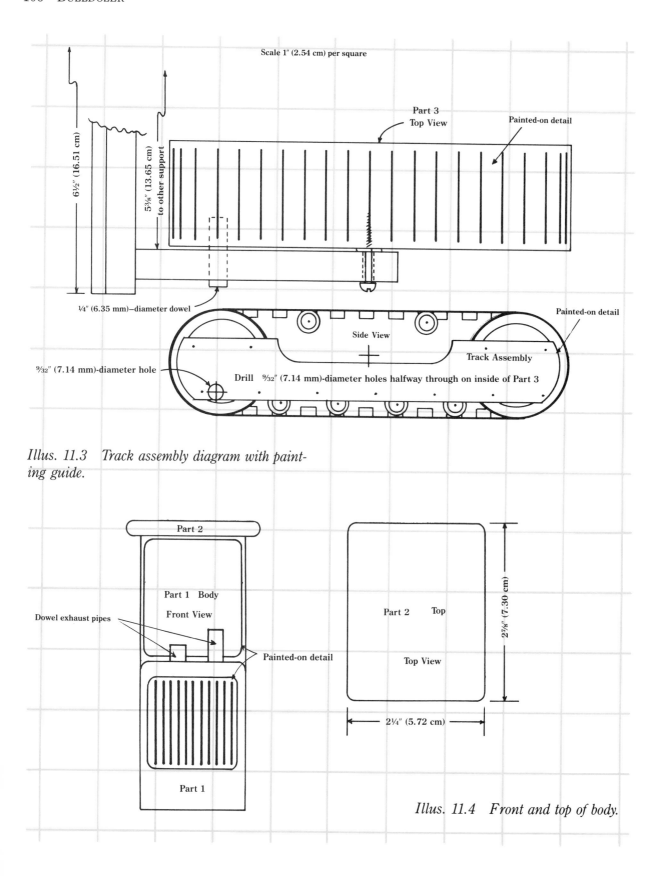

Scale 1″ (2.54 cm) per square

6½″ (16.51 cm)

5⅜″ (13.65 cm)

to other support

Part 3
Top View

Painted-on detail

¼″ (6.35 mm)—diameter dowel

Painted-on detail

Side View

⁹⁄₃₂″ (7.14 mm)-diameter hole

Track Assembly

Drill   ⁹⁄₃₂″ (7.14 mm)-diameter holes halfway through on inside of Part 3

Illus. 11.3   Track assembly diagram with painting guide.

Part 2

Part 1   Body

Front View

Dowel exhaust pipes

Painted-on detail

Part 1

Part 2   Top

Top View

2⅞″ (7.30 cm)

2¼″ (5.72 cm)

Illus. 11.4   Front and top of body.

Illus. 11.5   Bulldozer track assembly with blade support peg installed.

TRACK ASSEMBLY

9. Locate and drill three ⁹⁄₃₂″ (7.14 mm) holes in each track assembly (Part 3). Two of these holes are on the inside of these parts and are designed to be the axle pivot holes for the rollers that will be installed later (Illus. 11.2). The other hole is on the outside near the front (Illus. 11.2 and 11.3). Drill each of these holes to a depth of ½″ (12.7 mm).

10. Cut two ¼″ (6.35 mm)-diameter dowel sections to a length of 1″ (2.54 cm).

11. Sand both ends of these dowels.

12. Glue them fully into the holes on the outside of Part 3. These pegs will support the bulldozer blade in its full-down position (Illus. 11.5).

13. Cut two 1″ (2.54 cm)-diameter dowel sections to 1⁵⁄₈″ (4.13 cm) length.

14. Locate the center at each end of these dowels and drill a ⁹⁄₃₂″ (7.14 mm) hole to a depth of ½″ (12.7 mm) into each end.

15. Cut four ¼″ (6.35 mm)-diameter dowel sections to 1″ (2.54 cm) lengths and sand well.

16. Glue the ¼″ (6.35 mm) dowels into the holes in the ends of the 1″ (2.54 cm) dowels (Illus. 11.6). These are the bulldozer's rollers.

17. Use carpenter's glue and ¾″ (19 mm) wire brads to assemble the top (Part 2) to the body (Part 1) as shown in Illus. 11.2 and 11.4.

18. Use glue and 2¼″ (5.72 cm) finishing nails to mount only one of the track assemblies (Part 3) to the body (Part 1). Use the dotted location marks in Illus. 11.2 to insure correct alignment.

19. Insert the rollers in place in their pivot holes and install the other track assembly (Part 3) in the same way (Illus. 11.7). NOTE: Do not glue the rollers.

20. Locate each fuel tank (Part 5) into place and secure with glue and 1¾″ (4.45 cm) finishing nails.

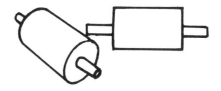

Illus. 11.6   Rollers with axles installed.

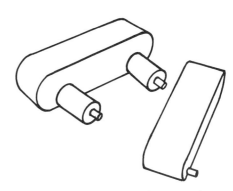

Illus. 11.7   Rollers operate between the two track assemblies.

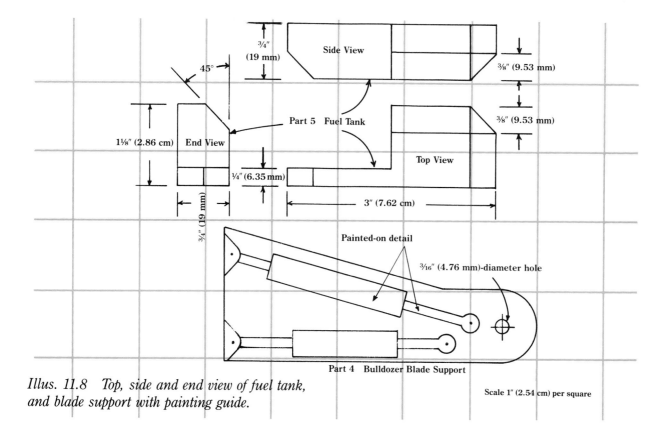

Illus. 11.8   Top, side and end view of fuel tank, and blade support with painting guide.

Scale 1″ (2.54 cm) per square

Illus. 11.9   Bulldozer blade and support assembly.

BLADE ASSEMBLY

21. Locate and drill the $\frac{3}{16}$″ (4.76 mm) pivot hole into each of the bulldozer blade supports (Part 4) (Illus. 11.6).
22. Use glue and $1\frac{3}{4}$″ (4.45 cm) finishing nails to assemble the bulldozer blade (Part 6) and supports (Part 4) (Illus. 11.2, 11.3 and 11.9).
23. Use the No. 8 roundhead woodscrews to install the blade assembly into place. Place the flat washers between Parts 3 and 4 to act as a bearing/spacer (Illus. 11.1).
24. Fill all nail holes.
25. Do any touch-up painting that might be necessary at this time.

Your Bulldozer is now complete and ready to begin its first major construction job.

Backhoe

Materials List

1¾" (4.45 cm)-thick hardwood, 6" × 15" (15.24 cm × 38.1 cm)

¾" (19 mm)-thick hardwood, 2½" × 12" (6.35 cm × 30.48 cm)

⅜" (9.53 mm)-thick veneer
plywood . . . . 1 square foot (3 square meters)

Hardwood dowel:
   ¼" (6.35 mm) diameter . . 12" (30.48 cm)
   ⅜" (9.53 mm) diameter . . 2" (5.08 cm)
   ½" (12.7 mm) diameter . . 18" (45.72 cm)
No. 8 1½" (3.81 cm)
   roundhead woodscrews . . . 2
No. 8 flat washers 6
No. 8 × 1¾" (4.45 cm)
   roundhead machine screws, 1
No. 8 machine nut 1
Hardwood toy wheels:
   1½" (3.81 cm) diameter . . 2
   2¼" (5.72 cm) diameter . . 2
Carpenter's glue . . . . small container
1½" (3.81 cm) finishing nails, small box
¾" (19 mm) wire brads . . . . small box
Nontoxic paint: your color choice in small containers

Cutting List

Part 1 . . . Body . . . . Make 1
Part 2 . . . Cab . . . . Make 1
Part 3 . . . Top . . . . Make 1
Part 4 . . . Fender . . . . Make 2
Part 5 . . . Rear Shovel Arm . . . . . . Make 1
Part 6 . . . Rear Shovel Side . . . . . . Make 2
Part 7 . . . Rear Shovel Bottom . . . . Make 1

Illus. 11.10

Part 8 . . . Forward Shovel Frame . . Make 2
Part 9 . . . Forward Shovel Back . . Make 1
Part 10 . . Forward Shovel Bottom, Make 1

Instructions

LAYOUT

1. Lay out and cut the profile (side view) of the tractor body (Part 1) from a piece of 1¾" (4.45 cm)-thick hardwood stock (Illus. 11.11).
   NOTE: Maple stock is recommended for this part because of its strength.
2. Cut the ¹³⁄₁₆" (20.6 mm) notch into the rear shovel support of Part 1 as indicated in Illus. 11.11 and 11.12.
3. Taper the sides of the rear shovel support as shown in Illus. 11.12.

ENGINE

4. Locate and drill the two holes into the top of the engine hood area. Drill to a depth of ¼" to ½" (6.35 mm to 12.7 mm). These holes are ¼" (6.35 mm) and ⅜" (9.53 mm) in diameter (Illus. 11.11 and 11.12).
5. Cut a ¼" (6.35 mm)-diameter dowel section to a length of ¾" (19 mm) and glue this dowel section fully into the ¼" (6.35 mm)

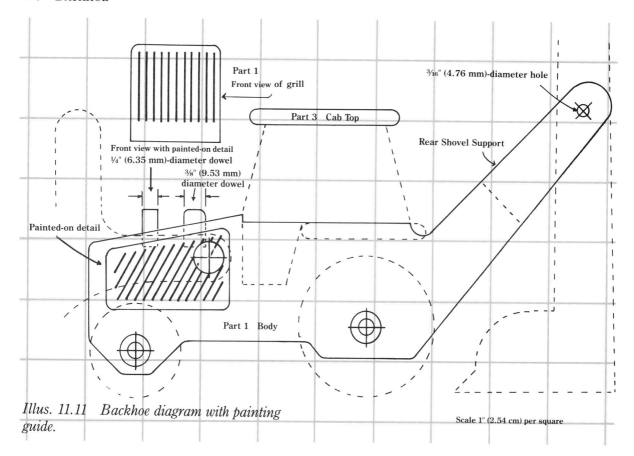

Illus. 11.11   Backhoe diagram with painting guide.

hole in the top of the engine hood area of the tractor body (Part 1). This dowel represents the tractor's exhaust pipe (Illus. 11.11 and 11.12).

6. Likewise, cut a ⅜″ (9.53 mm)-diameter dowel section to a ¾″ (19 mm) length and glue this one fully into the ⅜″ (19 mm) hole in the engine hood area of Part 1. Round the exposed end of this dowel lightly with sandpaper. This is the engine's air filter (Illus. 11.11 and 11.12).

7. To make the detail painting of this part easier, the entire part, including the detail painting, should be completely painted at this time (Illus. 11.11, 11.12 and 11.13).

REAR SHOVEL SUPPORT

8. Locate and drill the ³⁄₁₆″ (4.76 mm) hole in the top of the rear shovel support (Illus. 11.11).

9. Mark the location of each of the axle holes

and the forward shovel pivot/support (Illus. 11.11).

10. Using a ⁹⁄₃₂″ (7.14 mm) drill bit, drill completely through Part 1 at these three marks.

NOTE: Use a drill press or some other method to insure that these holes are drilled straight through the part, not at an angle.

11. Now change to a ½″ (12.7 mm)-diameter drill bit and drill out each of these holes on both sides of Part 1 to a depth of exactly ½″ (12.7 mm) (Illus. 11.12).

12. Cut six sections of ½″ (12.7 mm)-diameter dowel to 1″ (2.54 cm) lengths. Sand both ends of each dowel section.

13. Glue three of these dowel sections into the ½″ (12.7 mm) holes drilled in Step 11.

NOTE: Do Step 13 only on one side of Part 1 at this time.

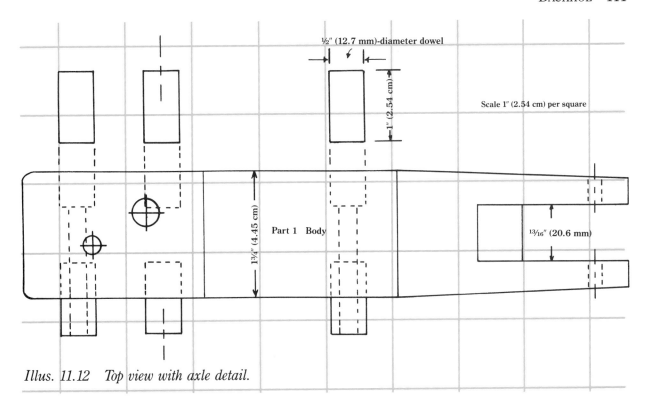

½″ (12.7 mm)-diameter dowel

1″ (2.54 cm)

Scale 1″ (2.54 cm) per square

Part 1   Body

1¾″ (4.45 cm)

13⁄16″ (20.6 mm)

Illus. 11.12   Top view with axle detail.

14. After the glue has dried completely, use the 9⁄32″ (7.14 mm) drill bit and back-drill from the opposite side of Part 1 through the ½″ (12.7 mm) dowel spacers, in the two axle holes only (Illus. 11.12 and 11.14).

15. Now glue the remaining three dowel sections into the ½″ (12.7 mm) holes on the other side of Part 1. Again, allow the glue to dry completely.

16. Back-drill again, through the axle holes only, with a 9⁄32″ (7.14 mm) drill bit completing the axle hole through Part 1 and the wheel-to-body spacers on each side.

CAB

17. To build the cab (Part 2 in Illus. 11.15), you will need a block of hardwood that measures approximately 3″ (7.62 cm) on all sides. This block can be obtained by laminating several thinner sections together.

18. Lay out and cut the profile of the tractor cab (Part 2) on this block (Illus. 11.15).

Illus. 11.13   Backhoe body with detail painting completed.

Illus. 11.14   Back-drill to continue axle holes through spacers.

Illus. 11.15 | *Front and side views of cab.*

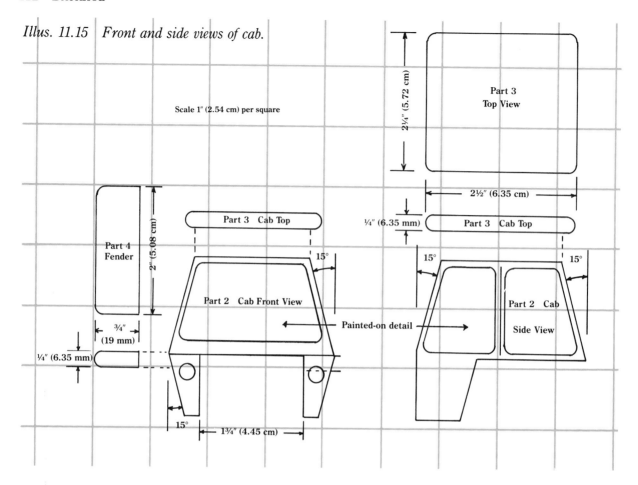

Scale 1″ (2.54 cm) per square

19. Now draw and cut the front view in a like manner (Illus. 11.15 and 11.16).
20. Again, the detail painting will be easier if the complete part is painted at this time. NOTE: The window glass has a more realistic look if the windows are painted white and slashed with silver streaks (Illus. 11.16).
21. Lay out and cut the cab top (Part 3) and the two fenders (Part 4) (Illus. 11.15).
22. Install the cab top (Part 3) to the cab (Part 2) with glue and wire brads (Illus. 11.15).
23. Assemble the cab (Part 2) into place on the tractor body (Part 1) and secure with glue and 2″ (5.08 cm) finishing nails.
24. Secure the fenders (Part 4) in place at the base of the cab with glue and wire brads (Illus. 11.15 and 11.17).

REAR SHOVEL

25. Lay out and cut the rear shovel arm (Part 5) from ¾″ (19 mm) hardwood stock (Illus. 11.18).
26. Drill the 3/16″ (4.76 mm) pivot hole and the ½″ (12.7 mm) handle hole as indicated in Illus. 11.18.
27. Cut two rear shovel sides (Part 6) and one rear shovel bottom (Part 7) from 3/8″ (9.53 mm) stock.
28. Assemble Parts 5, 6 and 7 of the rear shovel using glue and wire brads (Illus. 11.18 and 11.19).
29. Cut a section of ½″ (12.7 mm)-diameter hardwood dowel to a length of 4″ (10.16 cm).
30. Center this ½″ (12.7 mm) dowel section into the ½″ (12.7 mm) handle hole at the

Illus. 11.16   Backhoe cab with detail painting completed.

Illus. 11.17   Backhoe with cab, top and fenders installed.

Illus. 11.18   Front and side views of shovels.

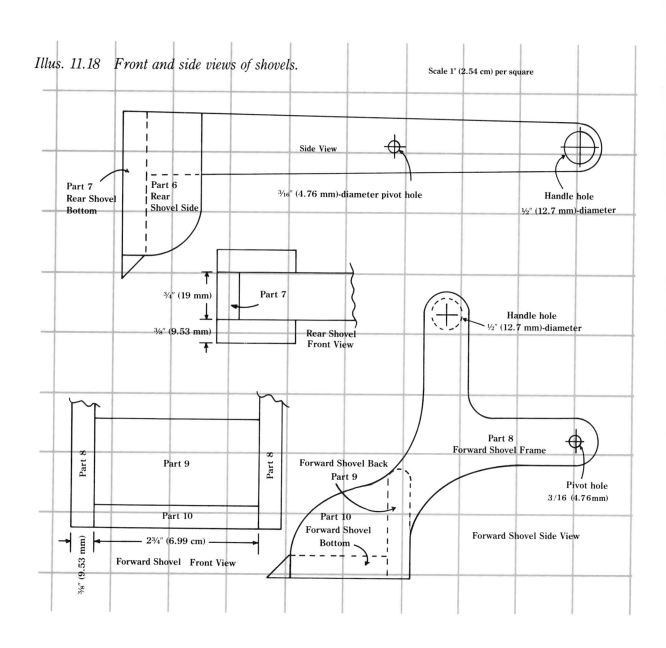

Scale 1″ (2.54 cm) per square

Side View

Part 7
Rear Shovel
Bottom

Part 6
Rear
Shovel Side

³⁄₁₆″ (4.76 mm)-diameter pivot hole

Handle hole
½″ (12.7 mm)-diameter

¾″ (19 mm)

Part 7

³⁄₈″ (9.53 mm)

Rear Shovel
Front View

Handle hole
½″ (12.7 mm)-diameter

Part 8

Part 9

Part 8

Part 10

Forward Shovel Back
Part 9

Part 10
Forward Shovel
Bottom

Part 8
Forward Shovel Frame

Pivot hole
3/16 (4.76mm)

Forward Shovel Side View

³⁄₈″ (9.53 mm)

2¾″ (6.99 cm)

Forward Shovel   Front View

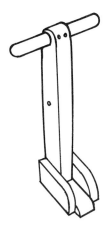

Illus. 11.19   Rear shovel assembly.

Illus. 11.20   Forward shovel assembly.

top of the rear shovel arm (Part 5) and secure with glue and wire brads (Illus. 11.19).

FORWARD SHOVEL

31. Lay out and cut two of the forward shovel frame (Part 8) from ⅜″ (9.53 mm) veneer plywood (Illus. 11.18).

32. Locate and drill the ³⁄₁₆″ (4.76 mm) pivot hole and the ½″ (12.7 mm) handle hole as shown in Illus. 11.18.

33. Cut one forward shovel back (Part 9) and forward shovel bottom (Part 10) as shown in Illus. 11.18.

34. Assemble the forward shovel as shown in Illus. 11.18, using glue and 1½″ (3.81 cm) finishing nails (Illus. 11.20).

35. Cut a section of ½″ (12.7 mm)-diameter dowel to a length of 3½″ (8.89 cm) and install it into the handle holes of the forward shovel. Use glue and wire brads to secure in place (Illus. 11.20).

AXLES

36. Cut two ¼″ (6.35 mm) dowel sections to 3¾″ (9.53 cm) in length. These are the tractor's axles.

37. Insert these axle sections through the axle holes of the tractor body (Part 1).

38. Secure the two 2¼″ (5.72 cm)-diameter hardwood toy wheels to the rear axle and the two 1½″ (3.81 cm)-diameter hardwood toy wheels to the forward axle with carpenter's glue (Illus. 11.10).

NOTE: Be careful not to allow the glue to get into the axle holes.

FINISHING

39. Mount the rear shovel assembly to the rear shovel support arm with a No. 8 × 1¾″ (4.45 cm) roundhead machine screw and No. 8 machine nut. Use No. 8 flat washers as necessary, for bearing surfaces (Illus. 11.10).

40. Install the forward shovel assembly to the forward shovel pivot/support spacers with a No. 8 roundhead woodscrew on each side. Use No. 8 flat washers for bearing surfaces as necessary (Illus. 11.10).

41. Fill all nail holes with wood filler.

42. Touch-up and complete the painting as necessary.

The Back Hoe is now finished.

Construction Digger

Materials List

1½" (3.81 cm)-thick hardwood, 5" × 20" (12.7 cm × 50.8 cm)

¾" (19 mm)-thick hardwood, 5" × 15" (12.7 cm × 38.1 cm)

Hardwood dowel:
- ¼" (6.35 mm) .... 2" (5.08 cm)
- ¾" (19 mm) .... 6" (15.24 cm)

No. 8 × 1½" (3.81 cm)
    roundhead woodscrew 1
No. 8 × 1¾" (4.45 cm)
    roundhead machine screw .. 1
No. 8 machine nut 1
No. 8 flat washer 4
No. 8 fender washer 1
Carpenter's glue .... small container
2" (5.08 cm) finishing nails , small box
¾" (19 mm) wire brads ..... small box
Nontoxic paint: your color choice in small containers

Cutting List

Part 1 ... Body Side .... Make 2
Part 2 ... Body Center .... Make 1
Part 3 ... Track Assembly .... Make 2
Part 4 ... Boom Arm .... Make 1
Part 5 ... Track Assembly Spacer
                Block .... Make 1
Part 6 ... Shovel Arm .... Make 1
Part 7 ... Shovel Side .... Make 2
Part 8 ... Shovel Bottom .... Make 1
Part 9 ... Shovel Back .... Make 1

Instructions

BODY

1. Lay out and cut the three body parts (Parts 1

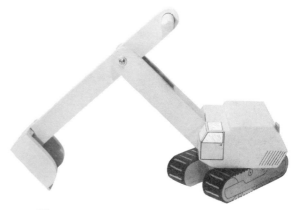

Illus. 11.21

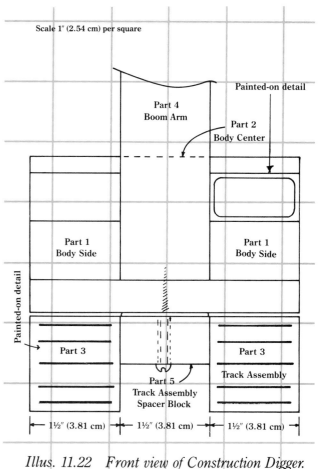

Illus. 11.22   Front view of Construction Digger.

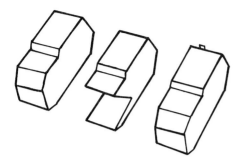

Illus. 11.23   Unassembled body parts for the Construction Digger.

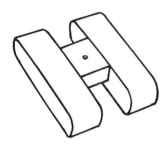

Illus. 11.24   Assembled track assembly.

and 2) from 1½″ (3.81 cm) stock. Cut two of the body sides (Part 1) and one of the body center (Part 2) (Illus. 11.22 and 11.26). NOTE: Part 2 is identical to Part 1 with the exception of the notch in the front that is designed for the boom arm (Part 4) to fit into (Illus. 11.22, 11.23 and 11.26 insert).

2. Lay out and cut to shape the boom arm (Part 4) from 1½″ (3.81 cm) stock (Illus. 11.27).

3. Locate and drill the ³⁄₁₆″ (4.76 mm) pivot hole in the top end of the boom arm (Part 4, Illus. 11.27).

4. Assemble Parts 1, 2 and 4 using carpenter's glue and 2″ (5.08 cm) finishing nails (Illus. 11.25).

5. Drill a ⁹⁄₃₂″ (7.14 mm) hole for the exhaust pipe at the rear of this assembly (Illus. 11.26). Drill to a depth of 1″ (2.54 cm).

6. Cut a section of ¼″ (6.35 mm)-diameter dowel to a length of 1½″ (3.81 cm). Cut this dowel at an angle of approximately 30°.

7. Sand each end of the dowel section and glue it fully into the hole drilled in Step 5. Turn the

dowel so that the beveled side faces away from the rear of the body assembly.

8. Detail painting is made easier if the painting is done before final assembly. Paint this assembly now.

NOTE: Windows should be painted white with silver slash marks to simulate glass.

TRACK

9. Lay out and cut to shape two of the track assembly (Part 3) from 1½″ (3.81 cm) stock (Illus. 11.22 and 11.26).

10. The track assembly spacer block (Part 5) is a 1½″ × 2″ (3.81 cm × 5.08 cm) part cut from ¾″ (19 mm) stock (Illus. 11.22, 11.24 and 11.26).

11. **Drill a ³⁄₁₆″ (4.76 mm) hole through the center of the 1½″ × 2″ (3.81 cm × 5.08 cm) side of this block (Illus. 11.22 and 11.26).**

12. Assemble Parts 3 and 5 with glue and finishing nails (Illus. 11.24).

13. Paint the track assembly at this time.

14. Assemble the track assembly to the bottom of the body assembly as indicated in Illus. 11.26, using a roundhead woodscrew. Place a fender washer between the two wooden assemblies to act as a bearing pivot surface. NOTE: Tighten the screw enough to secure the parts together firmly, but not so tight as to prevent them from swiveling.

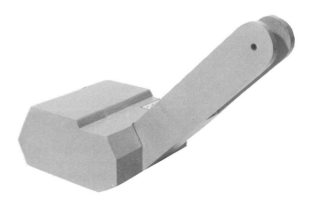

Illus. 11.25   Assembled body and boom of Construction Digger.

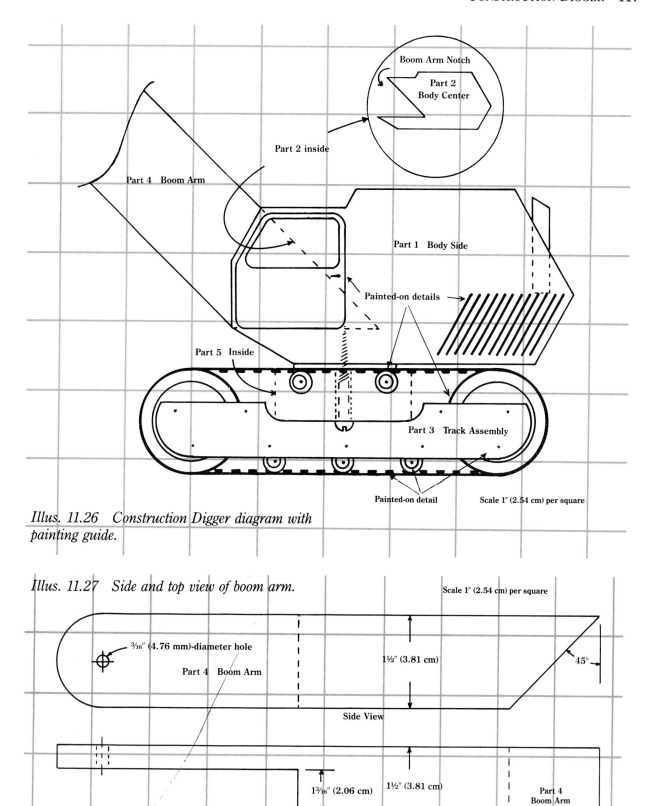

Illus. 11.26 Construction Digger diagram with painting guide.

Boom Arm Notch

Part 2
Body Center

Part 2 inside

Part 4 Boom Arm

Part 1 Body Side

Painted-on details

Part 5 Inside

Part 3 Track Assembly

Painted-on detail

Scale 1″ (2.54 cm) per square

Illus. 11.27 Side and top view of boom arm.

Scale 1″ (2.54 cm) per square

³⁄₁₆″ (4.76 mm)-diameter hole

Part 4 Boom Arm

1½″ (3.81 cm)

45°

Side View

1³⁄₁₆″ (2.06 cm)

1½″ (3.81 cm)

Part 4
Boom Arm

Top View

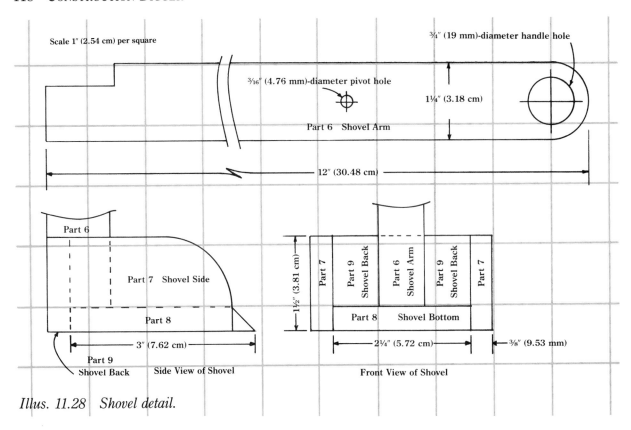

Scale 1″ (2.54 cm) per square

¾″ (19 mm)-diameter handle hole

³⁄₁₆″ (4.76 mm)-diameter pivot hole

1¼″ (3.18 cm)

Part 6   Shovel Arm

12″ (30.48 cm)

Part 6

Part 7   Shovel Side

Part 8

3″ (7.62 cm)

Part 9
Shovel Back   Side View of Shovel

1½″ (3.81 cm)

Part 7 | Part 9 Shovel Back | Part 6 Shovel Arm | Part 9 Shovel Back | Part 7

Part 8   Shovel Bottom

2¼″ (5.72 cm)   ⅜″ (9.53 mm)

Front View of Shovel

Illus. 11.28   Shovel detail.

SHOVEL

15. Lay out and cut the shovel arm (Part 6) from ¾″ (19 mm) stock (Illus. 11.28).

16. Locate and drill the ³⁄₁₆″ (4.76 mm) pivot hole and the ¾″ (19 mm) handle hole through this part (Illus. 11.28).

17. Lay out and cut to shape two shovel sides (Part 7), one shovel bottom (Part 8), and one shovel back (Part 9). Rip some ¾″ (19 mm) stock to ⅜″ (9.53 mm) thickness to provide material for these parts (Illus. 11.28).

18. Cut a section of ¾″ (19 mm)-diameter dowel to a length of 4½″ (11.43 cm) for the shovel handle.

19. Sand all of the above parts to prepare for assembly.

20. Assemble the shovel (Parts 6, 7, 8 and 9) using glue and wire brads (Illus. 11.28 and 11.29).

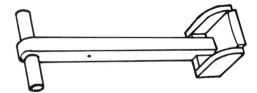

Illus. 11.29   Shovel assembly for the Construction Digger.

21. Center the shovel handle through the ¾″ (19 mm) hole provided and secure with glue and wire brads (Illus. 11.29).

22. Paint the shovel assembly at this time. Also do any touch-up painting on the main assembly that might be necessary.

23. Mount the shovel assembly to the boom arm with a machine screw and nut (Illus. 11.21).

    NOTE: Use flat washers as necessary to serve as bearings or spacers.

The Construction Digger is ready to join the other machines on the construction site.

Dump Truck

Materials List

1¾" (4.45 cm)-thick hardwood, 3" × 8" (7.62 cm × 20.32 cm)

¾" (19 mm)-thick hardwood stock .... 5" × 15" (12.7 cm × 38.1 cm)

⅜" (9.53 mm)-thick veneer plywood .... 10" × 20" (25.4 cm × 50.8 cm)

1⅝" (4.13 cm)-diameter hardwood toy wheels 10

¼" (6.35 mm) diameter hardwood dowel .... 12" (30.48 cm)

1½" (3.81 cm) butt hinge ... 1

Carpenter's glue .... small container

1½" (3.81 cm) finishing nails, small box

¾" (19 mm) wire brads ..... small box

Nontoxic paint: your color choice in small containers

Cutting List

Part 1 ... Truck Chassis .... Make 1
Part 2 ... Front Axle Retainer .... Make 1
Part 3 ... Rear Axle Retainer .... Make 1
Part 4 ... Truck Cab .... Make 1
Part 5 ... Hood .... Make 1
Part 6 ... Right Fender .... Make 1
Part 7 ... Left Fender .... Make 1
Part 8 ... Dump Bed Side .... Make 2
Part 9 ... Dump Bed Front ...... Make 1
Part 10 .. Dump Bed Bottom .... Make 1
Part 11 .. Dump Bed Cab Protector, Make 1
Part 12 .. Dump Bed Tail Gate ... Make 1

Illus. 11.30

Instructions

LAYOUT

1. Lay out and cut to shape one truck chassis (Part 1), the front axle retainer (Part 2), and the rear axle retainer (Part 3) from ¾" (19 mm) hardwood stock (Illus. 11.32).

2. Sand these parts to prepare them for assembly.

3. Assemble the truck chassis (Part 1) and the axle retainers (Parts 2 and 3) using carpenter's glue and wire brads (Illus. 11.32 and 11.34).
   NOTE: Do not allow glue to get into the axle slots of Parts 2 and 3.

4. Lay out and cut to shape the truck cab (Part 4), the hood (Part 5) and both fenders (Parts 6 and 7) from 1¾" (4.45 cm) hardwood stock (Illus. 11.31).

5. Sand all of these parts well to prepare them for assembly.

6. Use Illus. 11.33 as a guide and locate Parts 4 and 5 in place on the truck chassis (Part 1). Secure them with glue and finishing nails (Illus. 11.35).

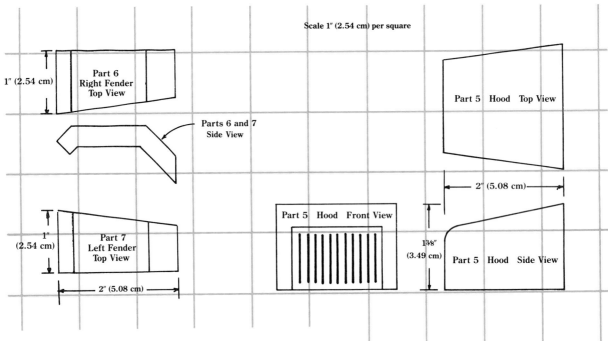

Scale 1″ (2.54 cm) per square

7. Install the fenders (Parts 6 and 7) to each side of the hood assembly with glue and finishing nails. Pre-drill nail holes to eliminate the possibility of splitting (Illus. 11.34 and 11.35).

8. Lay out and cut two dump-bed sides (Part 8) and one each of the other dump-bed parts (Parts 9, 10, 11 and 12) from ⅜″ (9.53 mm) veneer plywood (Illus. 11.36).

9. Sand all of these parts well.

ASSEMBLY

10. Assemble the dump-bed front, bottom and cab protector (Parts 9, 10 and 11) to the dump-bed sides (Part 8) using carpenter's glue and wire brads (Illus. 11.36 and 11.37).

11. Install the tailgate (Part 12) with one finishing nail on each side. This will allow it to hinge open. Pre-drill these holes to prevent splitting.

NOTE: Be sure the finishing nails are each ³⁄₁₆″ (4.76 mm) from the top so the tailgate will hinge correctly (Illus. 11.37).

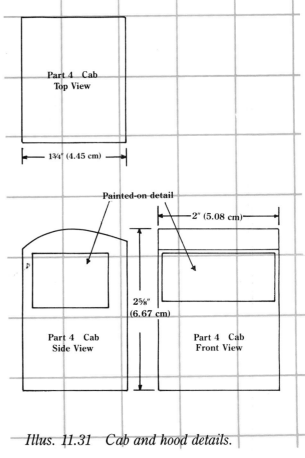

Illus. 11.31 Cab and hood details.

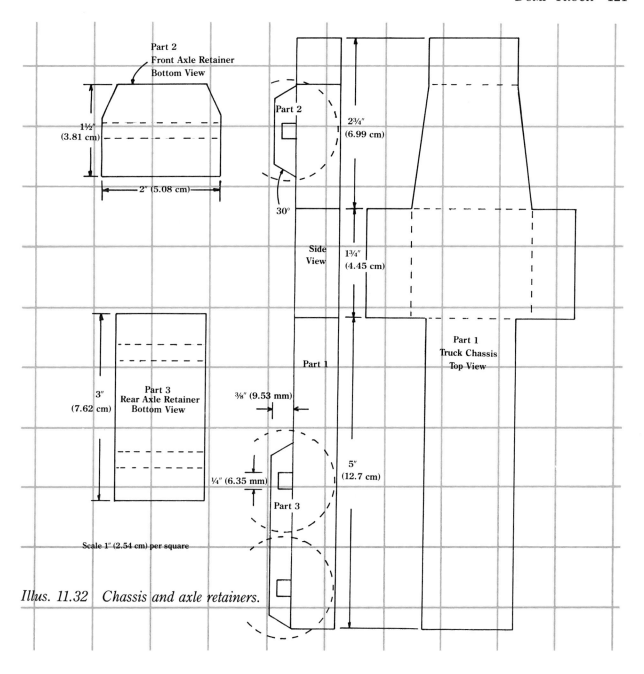

Illus. 11.32 Chassis and axle retainers.

12. Mount the dump-bed assembly to the truck chassis assembly by the use of a small butt hinge at the rear (Illus. 11.30).

13. Cut three sections of ¼″ (6.35 mm)-diameter dowel to 3½″ (8.89 cm) lengths. These are the truck's axles.

14. Insert these axles through the axle slots on the front and rear axle retainers.

15. Install 1⅝″ (4.13 cm)-diameter wooden toy wheels to these axles with a drop of glue. Do not allow glue to get into the axle retainer slots. The rear axles will require two wheels on each end. Refer to Chapter 3 if you prefer to build your own wheels.

16. Paint the entire project with nontoxic paint of your color choice.

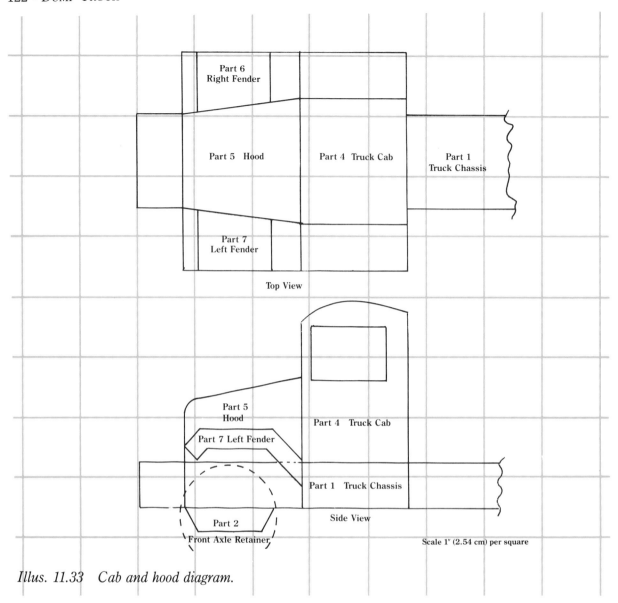

Part 6
Right Fender

Part 5   Hood

Part 4 Truck Cab

Part 1
Truck Chassis

Part 7
Left Fender

Top View

Part 5
Hood

Part 4   Truck Cab

Part 7 Left Fender

Part 1   Truck Chassis

Part 2

Side View

Front Axle Retainer

Scale 1″ (2.54 cm) per square

Illus. 11.33   Cab and hood diagram.

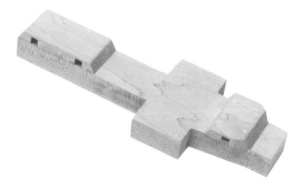

Illus. 11.34   Truck chassis with axle retainers installed.

Illus. 11.35   Truck chassis with cab, hood and fenders installed.

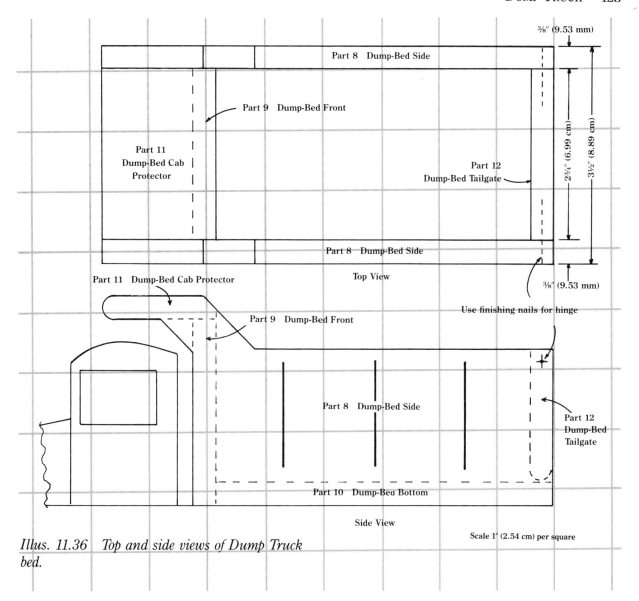

⅜" (9.53 mm)

Part 8   Dump-Bed Side

Part 9   Dump-Bed Front

Part 11
Dump-Bed Cab
Protector

Part 12
Dump-Bed Tailgate

2¾" (6.99 cm)

3½" (8.89 cm)

Part 8   Dump-Bed Side

Top View

Part 11   Dump-Bed Cab Protector

Part 9   Dump-Bed Front

⅜" (9.53 mm)

Use finishing nails for hinge

Part 8   Dump-Bed Side

Part 12
Dump-Bed
Tailgate

Part 10   Dump-Bed Bottom

Side View

Scale 1" (2.54 cm) per square

Illus. 11.36   Top and side views of Dump Truck bed.

17. The windows are to be painted white with silver slash marks to give the appearance of glass.

The Dump Truck is now complete and can be used for the first load of gravel to be delivered to the building site.

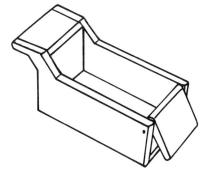

Illus. 11.37   Dump Truck bed assembly.

Road Grader

Materials List

1³⁄₄" (4.45 cm) hardwood ... 5" × 10" (12.7 cm × 25.4 cm)

³⁄₄" (19 mm) hardwood ..... 5" × 24" (12.7 cm × 60.96 cm)

Hardwood dowel:
  ¼" (6.35 mm) .... 22" (55.88 cm)
  ³⁄₈" (9.53 mm) .... 3" (7.62 cm)
  ½" (12.7 mm) .... 1" (2.54 cm)
2" (5.08 cm)-diameter hardwood toy wheels 6
Carpenter's glue .... small container
2" (5.08 cm) finishing nails .. small box
1½" (3.81 cm) finishing nails, small box
³⁄₄" (19 mm) wire brads ..... small box
Nontoxic paint: your color choices in small containers

Cutting List

Part 1 ... Forward Chassis ...... Make 1
Part 2 ... Cab and Engine Unit .. Make 1
Part 3 ... Cab Top .... Make 1
Part 4 ... Rear Axle Assembly .... Make 2
Part 5 ... Forward Axle Assembly, Make 1
Part 6 ... Grader Blade Mounting
                Block .... Make 1
Part 7 ... Grader Blade Retaining
                Ring .... Make 1
Part 8 ... Grader Blade .... Make 1

Illus. 11.38

Instructions

LAYOUT

1. Lay out and cut the forward chassis (Part 1) from ³⁄₄" (19 mm) hardwood stock (Illus. 11.39).
2. Drill the ⁹⁄₃₂" (7.14 mm) rear-axle assembly mounting hole and the ¹³⁄₃₂" (10.3 mm) grader-blade assembly mounting hole as indicated in Illus. 11.39.
3. Sand Part 1 to prepare it for assembly.
4. Lay out and cut the cab and engine unit (Part 2) to shape from 1³⁄₄" (4.45 cm) hardwood stock (Illus. 11.40).

CAB AND ENGINE

5. Drill the ¼" (6.35 mm) exhaust-pipe hole and the ½" (12.7 mm) air-cleaner hole in

Illus. 11.39   Part 1, forward chassis.

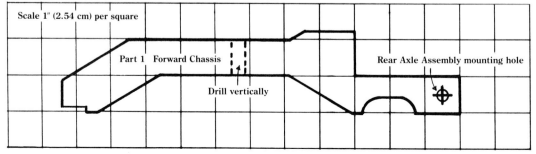

Scale 1" (2.54 cm) per square

Part 1 Forward Chassis

Drill vertically

Rear Axle Assembly mounting hole

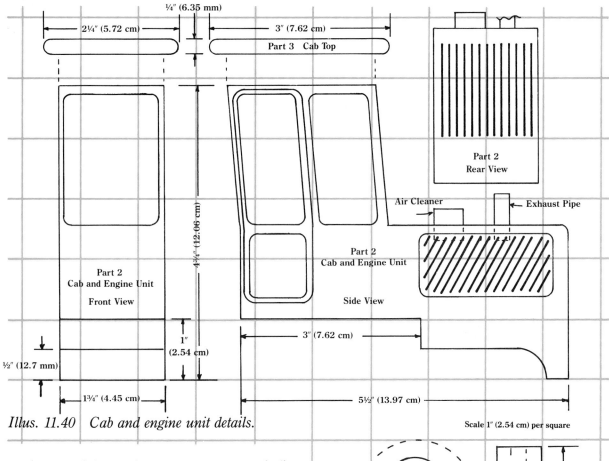

Illus. 11.40   Cab and engine unit details.

Scale 1″ (2.54 cm) per square

the top of the engine compartment, as indicated in Illus. 11.40. Drill these holes to a depth of ¼″ (6.35 mm).

6. Cut a section of ¼″ (6.35 mm)-diameter dowel to a length of ¾″ (19 mm). Sand both ends and glue it fully into the ¼″ (6.35 mm) hole in the top of the engine compartment.

7. In the same way, cut a section of ½″ (12.7 mm)-diameter dowel to a length of ½″ (12.7 mm), sand it well and glue it into the ½″ (12.7 mm) hole in the top of the engine compartment (Illus. 11.40).

8. Fabricate the cab top (Part 3) from a piece of ¾″ (19 mm) material by first ripping a ¼″ (6.35 mm)-thick slab. Then cut Part 3 to its finished dimensions of 2¼″ × 3″ (5.72 cm × 7.62 cm) (Illus. 11.40).

9. Sand it well, rounding the edges as shown in Illus. 11.40.

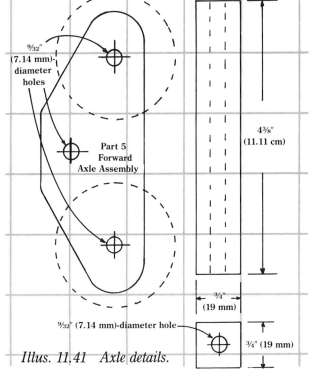

Illus. 11.41   Axle details.

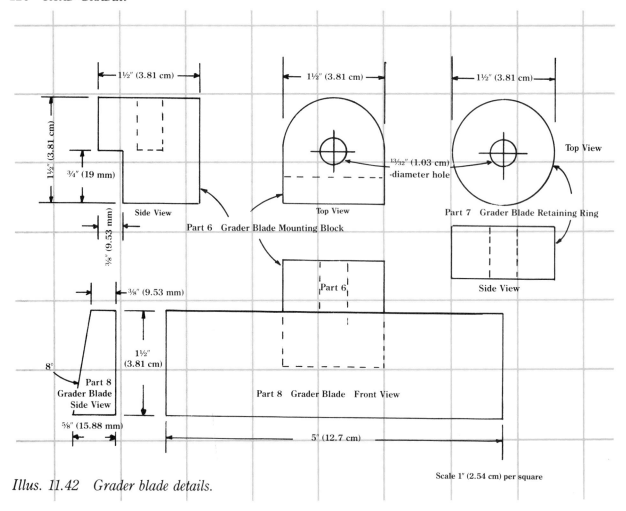

Illus. 11.42   Grader blade details.

10. Install the cab top (Part 3) to the cab and engine unit (Part 2) as indicated in Illus. 11.40. Use carpenter's glue and wire brads to secure it in place.

11. Paint the cab and engine unit prior to any further assembly to make the detail painting easier (Illus. 11.43). Also paint the forward chassis (Part 1) at this time.

CHASSIS

12. Assemble the forward chassis (Part 1) to the cab and engine unit assembly with glue and finishing nails (Illus. 11.44).

13. Lay out and cut the forward axle assembly (Part 5) and two of the rear axle assemblies (Part 4) from ¾″ (19 mm) stock (Illus. 11.41).

14. Drill the 9⁄32″ (7.14 mm) axle holes through these parts.

NOTE: Be sure the axle hole is drilled *straight* through the forward axle assembly (Part 5).

15. Cut one section of ¼″ (6.35 mm)-diameter dowel to a length of 3⅝″ (9.2 cm).

16. Insert this dowel section through the 9⁄32″ (7.14 mm) hole at the rear of the forward chassis assembly (Part 1).

17. Glue a rear axle assembly (Part 4) to each end of this dowel using the center mounting hole (Illus. 11.45).

NOTE: Make sure the rear axle assemblies (Part 4) are properly aligned as the glue sets.

18. Center the forward axle assembly (Part 5) in place at the front end of the forward chassis assembly (Part 1) and secure in place with glue and 1½″ (3.81 cm) finishing nails. Pre-drill the nail holes to prevent splitting.

    NOTE: Do not drill or nail through the center axle hole.

19. Cut three ¼″ (6.35 mm)-diameter dowel sections to a length of 4¾″ (12.07 cm).

20. Insert these dowel sections through the three axle holes and glue a 2″ (5.08 cm)-diameter hardwood toy wheel to each end.

BLADE

21. Lay out and cut the grader-blade mounting block (Part 6) from 1¾″ (4.45 cm) hardwood stock (Illus. 11.42).

22. Lay out and cut the grader blade (Part 8) and the retainer ring (Part 7) from ¾″ (19 mm) stock (Illus. 11.42).

23. Drill the ¹³⁄₃₂″ (10.3 mm)-diameter holes in Parts 6 and 7 (Illus. 11.42).

24. Mount the grader blade (Part 8) to the mounting block (Part 6) with glue and wire brads.

25. Cut a section of ⅜″ (9.53 mm)-diameter dowel to 2½″ (6.35 cm) in length.

26. Glue this dowel section into the ¹³⁄₃₂″ (10.3 mm) hole in the top of the grader-blade mounting block (Part 6).

27. Install the blade assembly to the forward chassis assembly by inserting the dowel up through the ¹³⁄₃₂″ (10.3 mm) hole in the center of the chassis and then gluing the retainer ring (Part 7) to the top of the dowel (Illus. 11.38).

    NOTE: Do not allow glue to get into pivot hole and cause binding.

Illus. 11.43   Cab and engine unit of Road Grader with detail painting completed.

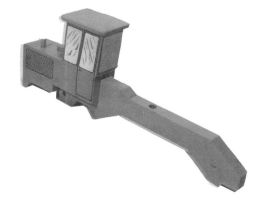

Illus. 11.44   Assemble the cab and engine unit to the forward chassis assembly.

Illus. 11.45   Installation of rear axle assembly.

28. Fill all nail holes and complete the painting process at this time.

This completes the Road Grader assembly.

Index